Options Trading Crash Course

The step-by-step guide, from beginner to advanced strategies, to create an additional online income stream and improve your life through options, swing and day trading

Simon Bord

professional before attempting any techniques outlined in this book.

By reading this document, the reader agrees that under no circumstances is the author responsible for any losses, direct or indirect, that are incurred as a result of the use of the information contained within this document, including, but not limited to, errors, omissions, or inaccuracies.

Table of Contents

Introduction

At the time of writing, untold scores of people are spending more time at home than ever, more out of necessity than choice. Listless hours are filled with all sorts of activities to keep the hands busy and the mind directed.

One of the most popular activities at the time of writing, which you may well have already attempted yourself, is options trading. It's insane how big the craze has gotten, almost as if it's the 21st century's analog to sports betting. But if you've tried trading for any length of time, you've likely realized that treating this hustle as a gamble is no way to pull out ahead consistently.

This isn't a day at the stables, or a night at the casino. You're not here to treat your money like it's part of a game. You're here to make it work for you, and achieve lasting financial freedom.

But maybe you've been struggling so far. Perhaps you feel options trading just isn't for you. Well, I'm here to help you find out whether or not that is actually true, as well as give you the best chance to succeed that I can.

A big reason why many people struggle to succeed with options trading is that they come in with the wrong mindset, and they don't have a mentor on hand to help them get out of it.

Trading, in some ways, is like fishing. You need patience. You need an inner calm, and a sense of composure. You need to be able to embrace the quiet, and resist the temptation to fiddle with your rod or play with your line just because your anxiety tells you to.

To get into that mindset where you can fit nicely into your metaphorical trading boat and ensure success, you first need to get off the hype train that led you, or at least many people with similar interests to you, into this field in the first place. You likely got here because of excitement and emotion, or perhaps a sense of unease, anxiety, or plain old peer pressure. These are perfectly normal things to feel, but there's a big difference between feeling an emotion and acting on it.

Trading, in action, is as calm and rational as it gets. This book is here to help you get off that mad hype train, that unstoppable engine with no brakes, and enjoy calmer, smoother sailing on richer waters. To start off, take a moment to breathe in deeply and relax, right now.

Now, how will this book help you relax? How will it help you become a better trader?

By making you not only more confident in this field, but more competent too. In the beginning, you'll find yourself walking through the utter basics of options trading. You'll learn why it's a thing that exists, how it works as a source of income, and more.

You'll be eased in with the simpler concepts, the key foundational basics that you need to get started, before also moving on to the more advanced tactics and strategies that you can try out.

Even more importantly, you'll be made aware of the most common mistakes an option trader can make. An entire chapter is dedicated to helping you spot pitfalls so that you don't need to get trapped by them. Now, you may cringe when you read some of them, especially if you've been trading for a while already, as you might recognize some of these pitfalls as things you already do. In these cases, do not stress. When a mistake is listed, it's only there so that you don't have to keep making it. The more you internalize and take to heart, the better you'll get at making wins. Even if you've been suffering under month after month of losses as a trader, you'll still be able to turn things around and make a success of this endeavor.

Some people have taken years before they started getting their successes reliably, so don't judge yourself based on your performance so far. However, we don't live in rainbow-unicorn land. So, it's important that we go about the build-up to your ultimate victory — your financial freedom and peace of mind — realistically. This isn't a get-rich-quick-scheme, and I don't recommend listening to anyone who urges you to treat this like one.

Ah, but why should you listen to me? I'll tell you upfront, I don't consider myself a top expert. However, I've put a lot of time and energy into research to get the income stream I have today, and I'm compiling that knowledge here now so that you can learn with ease many of the lessons I had to take in the hard way. Like I said, some people take years to learn. Others, months or weeks. This crash-course is here to help you condense some of that experience into a shorter period so you can start your smooth sailing sooner.

If you are set on options trading, you have nothing to lose from reading this, and everything to gain, and the price of this book is inconsequential compared to what you'll earn over time through the variety of solid, tried, and tested option-trading tactics written within.

As you learn these tactics, your knowledge of what you can do in trading will naturally expand. What you might not expect is that your knowledge of what the *market* can do will expand too. As you'll soon see, or may have already seen, the market can be a cruel and fickle paramour, but that doesn't mean that the relationship can't improve, or that the romance has to die.

As you get to know both yourself and the market better, you'll be able to act with greater decisiveness and maturity, even when under strain. You don't need to be rich to start or continue with this journey. Options trading is way, way cheaper to get into than stocks for example. However, that doesn't mean it stays cheap if you mess around.

On the flip side, once you know yourself, know what you're doing, know the market, and have a rough idea of what it *can* do, then not only will it stay cheap, but it'll become highly profitable too as you get better at reducing risks while maintaining rewards.

The sooner you start building this knowledge, the more value you'll be able to create with what you learn. There's no sense in sitting around waiting for inflation to claim your financial value, just as there's no sense waiting for entropy to cause the heat-death of the universe.

Give yourself permission to be bold, be brave, and start learning how to trade with options today!

But, one moment before we begin... let me just say thank you for joining me in this field, through this book. You'll be seeing a lot of what I think, but I want to hear what you think too! A review at any point is always appreciated. It keeps the conversation going.

Now, without any further ado...

Chapter 1: The Absolute Basics

The Reason We're Doing This: Financial Freedom

Before setting out to accomplish any goal, in this case achieving competency in options trading, it helps to have a clear reason. Something that keeps you grounded in reality, and allows you to pursue your strategy successfully without being pulled in by greed. In options trading, greed can be a form of entrapment that patsies you into a horrible loss, so anything to reduce its pull on you while still keeping you motivated to trade and succeed is good.

The specifics of this reason may vary from reader to reader, but I find in most cases that such reasons can be boiled down into one specific thing: financial freedom.

What is Financial Freedom Today?

Financial freedom is sometimes mistaken for the ability to do whatever the heck you want. While fulfilling your most important desires, or funding your most cherished goals is certainly part of financial freedom, this isn't all there is to it. Financial freedom means being able to tell quality from clutter, refusing to buy things just to satisfy a social pressure to fulfill an impulse. Financial freedom means being able to save your hard-earned money for what'll bring you long-term happiness. Generally, these things are not objects per se, but rather experiences. Especially experiences that you're able to share with those you care for most.

Financial freedom also involves knowing your means. Spending more than you earn in order to appear rich isn't financial freedom. Having lots of money doesn't intrinsically lead to financial freedom if you don't know what you're doing with it.

It's not about having a six-figure salary, it's about knowing where to put what you have (no matter how much or how little you have) in order to get the most value out of it. It's about having the will to set aside at least ten percent of what you earn for emergencies or your retirement, so that when a crisis strikes, or when you get too old to work your butt off, you'll be in a much better position to get through it without needing much (if any) money from anyone else.

That is financial freedom. Not necessarily to do whatever you want, whenever you want (because what you want will always change), but rather to fulfill what matters to you most without indebting yourself to people who only want to squeeze profit out of you. Through this kind of freedom, you can gain satisfaction, rather than chasing some consumer-crazed hunger that never goes away.

Aiming to satisfy every single impulse you might have, without consideration for your values (what matters to you on an emotional and intellectual level), only makes you a slave to those impulses. This can lead to financial slavery.

What is Financial Slavery?

In its simplest form, financial slavery can be summed up as debt.

Now, not every form of debt automatically leads to financial slavery. For instance, taking a loan to buy a property that you can then rent won't lead to financial slavery... assuming you already have reliable tenants lined up to live on that property. A pretty big assumption, to be fair.

Financial slavery is any debt that makes you feel like you're working to beat back the interest rates, rather than working to make your life better. When enslaved in this way, you're afraid to leave a job even when it's killing you because you cannot escape the question, "How am I going to pay off my mounting debt?"

Though you might even have a better job on the horizon, you may feel too afraid to let that debt keep accruing for any length of time where you don't have an income. This fear then leads to *fear-based* decisions that make it harder for you to live according to what you truly value.

On nights where you were particularly overworked, you may have even snapped at a loved one in frustration. At the time, you may have felt frustrated with them, but really you're frustrated with the situation you're in.

You might notice that you are already financially free in some ways, and enslaved in others. For instance, maybe you have a healthy savings account squirreled away, but are still fighting with debt. If you struggle to save more than a tenth of what you earn, using your savings to pay off your debt might not be feasible. This example is a sign that a little more money, coming in with some consistency, can really help you out.

So, the whole reason you're learning to be an options trader is to help give you the capital needed to get further away from financial slavery, and closer to financial freedom, so that your most important values and life-goals can have more time dedicated to them.

Key Methods to Start Building a Financial Freedom Mindset

Get a Budget Going

If you don't have one already, this is a must. This doesn't have to be anything complex. Most people already have a monthly budget, but I highly recommend you use a weekly one instead. Track how much you spend over the course of a week, counting every little purchase you make. Now, compare it to how much of your salary you've earned over the course of that week. Try to keep how much you're spending below the income value of your week.

Budgets are extremely helpful, as they help prevent you killing your finances with a death by a thousand cuts. They also help build a saving/ spending routine in you that can help preserve your willpower, allowing you to avoid impulse buys that don't bring much value into your life compared to the value you're giving up for them.

Don't Enter a Consumer Arms Race With Your Neighbor

Also often called, "Keeping up with the Joneses," where you buy something just to one-up or match an item possessed by someone in your street.

There's no prize for winning this kind of race. You don't get a gold medal for buying things just to stay ahead of your neighbors in terms of gadgets and the like, you just get a massive bill. You don't even get any meaningful social cred for it, at least not with anyone you'd want to rely on. The cred only lasts until someone else gets the next Cool Thing™, and the street stays financially enslaved.

Know Your Values

There are loads of free online guides as well as great self-care books that deal with this topic. Sites like Healthline, Mindtools, or Psychology Today are all great places to do a little soul-searching. Gaining a more conscious idea of what you want like this can help you decide whether or not a purchase is worth it.

If You're Not Sure, Come Back Tomorrow

If a purchase is tempting, but you're just on the edge on whether or not to buy it, rather come back the next day. Give the emotion a chance to wash over you and dissipate so you can come back with a more logical mind. Why do you think tourist shops are all overpriced? They know you won't be able to use the "come back tomorrow" tactic with them! Always use this tactic to avoid spending money you don't have on things you don't need, even when you know you might not be able to come back tomorrow. You'll live.

Know Your Limits

A good rule of thumb is that if you can't buy something twice without going broke, you can't afford it. Anything that expensive will either put you into debt, or uncomfortably close to it. Certainly not what we want for financial freedom. This is also a good cornerstone to bear in mind as part of your trading philosophy.

Treasure Experiences, Not Things

An object is only worth as much as what it can do for you. Regardless of how cheap or expensive it is, an object that only offers limited or short-term experiences usually won't have as good an impact on you as something that manages to provide lasting entertainment, impart a lifelong lesson, or create a happy memory. The quality of the experiences you get can't be intrinsically predicted by how big the price tag is. Paying for an escort, for example, isn't likely to be as good an experience as going with a cherished friend, relative, or lover, despite the escort being so much more expensive than those other options.

Save Before You Spend

Make sure you have at least some sort of bond, money market, or high-yield savings account that can cover your absolutely necessary living expenses for about half a year, give or take a month or two. I highly recommend using your budget to build such an account up before trading, even if it'll take you a while to do so. This is needed not only for your peace of mind, but also to enable patience. Speaking of patience...

Build Patience, and Never Raise Stakes Out of Greed

This will be elaborated on later in the book, as the balance of patience and greed is critical to successful options trading in particular, not just financial freedom overall. However, it does not hurt to introduce patience as one of your core values early on, as patience is what helps a trader succeed.

Important Terms and Distinctions

Trading vs. Investing

As someone in options trading, you might think you'll just be a trader. However, there is no need to put yourself in a pigeon-hole. When trading in options, you'll be working with both traders and investors, and you'll fall somewhere on a spectrum between them.

Let's first cover what an investor is. An investor:

- Spends money in return for stocks, bonds and other assets
- They usually hold these assets for years, if not decades
- They focus heavily on long-term gain, not fussed much by day-to-day fluctuations in the market, knowing things will normalize again soon enough

- Care more about the management of whatever they're investing in
- Doesn't care much about market news or reports
- Will diversify by industry or asset class
- Can buy and hold investments for a mostly passive income stream

A trader, meanwhile...

- Also spends money on assets, but usually with the expectation that they'll sell them soon
- Some traders are content to wait years between buying and selling
- Swing traders will only wait a few days or weeks
- Day traders will never wait more than 24 hours
- Options traders will wait according to the terms of the options contract, and the state of the market
- Compared to investors, traders care much more about the state of the market, as it's much more likely to impact their overall profit
- Cares a lot about market news and reports
- Will diversify mostly according to option prices and durations
- Makes many transactions in a relatively short time period
- Can't really be 'passive' outside of covered calls, but they still work on their own terms, and have some flexibility over the pace they need to work

As you can see, if all you do is options trading, then you'll be much more of a trader than an investor. This book also focuses on being a trader. However, don't think that this then limits you to just being a trader. Trading requires more active work compared to investing, but in return you get a much more powerful income stream. You can then use part of that income to invest.

General Glossary

Key terms that appear throughout this book, <u>*underlined and in italics*</u>, can be found succinctly summed up here.

Options: contracts, essentially. Option contracts are legally attached to another asset, like a stock, bond, or raw material. This is what gives these contracts their value. If you own this contract, then you have the legal right to either buy or sell whatever asset is attached to it at a predetermined price, regardless of what the market does, so long as you do so before a specified date.

Calls: option contracts that give you the right to buy their attached assets at the promised price, so long as it's within the timeframe written on the contract. Regardless of what is written in later examples, a single call usually consists of 100 shares in the attached asset.

Puts: like calls, but this time it's a right to sell, not to buy. Regardless of what is written in later examples, a single put usually consists of 100 shares in the attached asset.

Premium: the amount of money you pay to own an option contract.

Strike Price: The amount you're entitled to buy or sell an asset for, according to your option contract.

American: An option that can be exercised at any point in time as long as it's before the expiry date. Is NOT necessarily an option written up in America. American calls will have 'CA' written in the contract, while American puts will have 'PA' instead.

European: An option that can only be exercised on its expiration date. Again, it is not necessarily an option that was written in Europe. European calls will have 'CE' written in the contract, while European puts will have 'PE' instead.

Volatile: adjective used to describe assets whose price may fluctuate rapidly to a large degree, such that the assets are considered riskier to trade or invest in.

In The Money: When a call's attached asset or underlying security (same thing) has a higher market value than its strike price. Also, when a put's attached asset has a *lower* market value compared to its strike price.

Backtesting: Testing your trading strategy using past (but still relevant) data to see how you'll perform over a period of time.

Slippage: The difference between the price you thought you were trading at compared to the price that you actually traded at. Can be positive or negative. This happens when a market is so volatile or fast-moving that the value of your trade request changes in the few seconds between it being sent and processed.

Execution Errors: Any human error you can make at any point of the trade (e.g. adding another zero to the end of the money you're willing to pay).

Long: Synonymous with 'bullish,' opposite of 'short' or 'bearish.' 'Long' simply means buying something because you believe its value will increase, whereas 'short' means selling something because you believe its value will go down.

Diversification: the act of holding a variety of different option types, rather than having multiple options of the same type, in order to reduce risk. Diversification means that if something goes wrong with one option type, you'll still be able to count on the other types you have at hand.

The 1-5% Rule: The rule that you should risk no more than 1-5% of your trading account's value in any one trade, so as to manage risk and keep losses under control. It also includes cut-off points for cases where you do lose: if you lose 2-3% of your value in a day, don't make any more trades that day. If you lose 4-5% or more within a week, don't make any more trades for that week. For the sake of your success, do not break these rules.

Chapter 2: Getting Started With Options

Understanding Options

To understand _options_, we need to open with a question that might seem a little philosophical, "Why do options exist? Why are they here?"

Below, we look at two common examples. They aren't the only examples in existence, but they tend to be the premise from which the rest evolve.

Options As Insurance

Options can be understood as a form of insurance. Let's say someone (we'll call them Fred) owns an asset, like stocks in Grammarly, but is afraid its value might drastically change within a certain period of time. Fred might then pay a _premium_ to have a _put_ written for them by a finance company.

All options contracts, whether _calls_ or puts, cost a premium.

Let's say these stocks are currently worth $20 per share. Let's also say Fred owns about 40 of these stocks. So, they're currently worth $800 in total. It might cost someone $80 to legally own a put that covers all 40 stocks and lasts for 1 year. Let's say the _strike price_ for this option is $15 per share.

Now, if the value of these stocks falls below $15, let's say as low as $5, and they don't look like their value will go up before the end of the year, Fred (thanks to his put) can still sell their stocks for $15 to the company that wrote that put.

So, instead of losing $600 of value from their stocks dropping from $20 each to $5 each, Fred only lost $200 ($280 if you include the premium paid for the put to begin with). A much better outcome than if Fred never purchased a put. If the value of these stocks somehow fell to $0 within the specified timeframe, that put would _still_ let Fred sell his stocks for $15 each regardless.

But what if the stock prices don't fall? What if they even grow?

Well, Fred doesn't have to sell their stocks for $15. When you buy an option contract you get a _right_, but not a _compulsion_ or _obligation_. If the value of Fred's stocks has risen, such as to a value of $25 or even $30, he can still sell his stocks for that full price. Sure, he's $80 poorer compared to if he never bought the put, but that's nothing compared to what he's just gained, so he doesn't mind.

So, an option is a great way to partially protect the value of assets you plan to sell for a relatively low cost.

Options As Income (Basic)

Now, let's say Fred has the same stocks as before, at that same $20 value each.

Fred may choose to increase the earnings of his (or her) stocks by writing an option and then selling that option to someone else. Here, Fred would write a call option, perhaps with a strike price of $25 per share.

Again, the premium Fred gets paid is $80 in our example. Again, we're going to say the option is valid for one year. Now, if that year ticks over, and the market never values Fred's stocks at higher than $25, then Fred's won. Fred just earned $80 for doing basically nothing. As a large proportion of options never get used (over 75% of those that lasted until expiration in the 1990s — Picardo, 2021), this is actually a highly likely outcome.

But what if the market does value these stocks higher than $25? What if the market even values them as high as $30 or $35? Well, then whoever Fred wrote and sold the call option contract to is going to immediately buy all 40 of Fred's Grammarly stocks for $25 each — less than the market says they're now worth — and then turn around and sell them for an instant, easy profit.

However, it doesn't have to get as high as $30; as long as the total value of the stocks is worth more than their total strike price plus their premium, whoever holds this call option will want to exercise their option rights to sell those stocks.

Needless to say, the more likely it is that those stocks will rise in value within the agreed timeframe, the higher Fred is going to make his premium. In real life, Fred is also unlikely to want to tie all his assets to a single option, as he (or she) wouldn't want them all to be sold off in one flurry of personal bad luck.

So, Overall, What Makes Options Profitable?

On An Immediate Level

If you're the one who bought the option (paid the premium), then it'll be profitable if:

- in the case of a call, the total market value of your option's assets is bigger than the total strike price of those assets plus the premium you paid
- note that, in the case of a put, you won't profit if you use it as insurance

  — instead, you'd have to sell your assets early on, then buy them back later after their value has gone down and everyone's looking to cut their losses and sell back (this is a relatively risky and advanced strategy to be covered in more depth later)

If you're the one who sold the option (wrote the contract), then it'll be profitable if:

- in the case of a call, the total market value of your option's assets never gets bigger than the total strike price plus the premium you charged
- in the case of a put, the market value of the option's assets doesn't remain lower than the striking price towards the expiration date

  — if, in the case of a put, the market value of those assets does remain lower, the person you wrote and sold the put to will likely exercise their legal right to have you buy those assets, in a climate where you can either keep them or sell them for a loss

Note that buying options is generally better for beginners due to the relatively low amounts of money you risk at any one time, however statistically speaking you'll earn more consistently from writing options than purchasing them. This is because in roughly 75% of cases the value of an asset never deviates enough from the strike price to make using a call or put option profitable to exercise.

So, in most cases, the person who pays the premium loses. However, when they win, they win much more in one go than the writer ever could, while the writer always has a much bigger potential risk than the buyer ever has to worry about. Whether you choose to write or buy depends on whether you prefer small consistent gains with the occasional big loss, or frequent small losses offset by immensely profitable gains.

In the Long Term

What makes options profitable in the long-term, assuming you have a well-tested strategy, is consistency and mental resilience. Right now, internalize that even with the best strategies you will lose money from time to time. If you're buying, you're likely to have losses for several months in a row from time to time. But that doesn't matter. When you have a working strategy, or a consistent selection of strategies that you employ in tandem, then on average you will profit. However, these losses are why I say you must have a budget; you must never spend more on buying month-long call options, for instance, than what you could comfortably lose each month anyways. Otherwise, the losses will drive you mad and you'll chicken out before your strategy pays off.

Likewise, you wouldn't want to write a put option if your budget or financial buffer zone couldn't comfortably handle actually buying the attached assets.

What Determines the Premium Value of an Option?

The Underlying or Attached Asset

As stated earlier, the value of the attached assets plays a huge role in how much an option is worth. However, not all options contracts are impacted equally by a change in value for an underlying asset.

If you ever wish to model the risks or scenarios around options trading mathematically (some traders get by without doing so, others find it essential), the impact that a change in your attached asset's value will have is traditionally represented by Delta (Δ). Meanwhile, the speed at which this asset's value changes can be represented with Gamma (Γ).

Duration

Typically speaking, the less time an option has before it expires, the less the premium tends to be. This is because the less time an option has, the less likely it'll ever become profitable for the buyer. Duration has a huge effect on _American_ options, but not as much on _European_ options. For European options, having a long duration is only really good for the buyer (with a higher premium to match) if it's believed the _difference between the strike price and market value_ will favor them by then.

When mathematically modeling an option trade, the impact that duration has on your trade is represented by the Theta (θ) symbol.

Difference Between Strike Price and Market Value

This is pretty common sense. As an example, a put buyer would find a put option more valuable if its strike price is already very close to (or even below) the current market value. For this reason, the writer can justify a higher premium to account for the riskier position they're starting in.

Volatility

If the market for an asset is _volatile_, then any options based on that asset will be inherently riskier. Volatility isn't a constant, but rather a measure that changes over time. When someone wishes to see how the change in volatility might impact the risk levels of their trade, they'll use Vega to try to work out how their option contract will respond to estimated changes in volatility.

Risks and Rewards

You aren't necessarily going to be someone who has stocks or similar assets, at least not yet, so now you may be wondering if options are still relevant to you. The answer is yes! Something you may have noticed is that buying a call or a put for a certain number of stocks is much cheaper than buying the stocks themselves.

Despite this, you still have the legal right to either buy or sell them. You have the legal right to either _own_ them or convert them into liquid cash whenever you wish. Because of this right, you're able to profit off the assets of others without _actually_ owning those assets. One example is by trading the options themselves.

Let's say you buy a call option. You pay a nice premium on it. While you can wait and see if the assets are valued highly enough on the market to warrant exercising your option's rights, you could also choose to _sell the option off to someone else instead,_ or perhaps trade it for an actual asset of some kind. As long as the value of what you're getting is greater than the premium you paid, you profit.

However, you may have been able to intuit that options tend to get less valuable as time goes on, since their duration naturally shrinks. This means your option needs to look like it'll be _in the money_ soon if you wish to sell it at a profit, which might not happen. But that is simply one of the risks of options trading.

The Key Reasons to Keep Trading Options — Aside From Hedging, Insurance, or Earning Premiums

While Options Trading is a good way to amass wealth, it isn't the only way. What advantages does it have that separates it from, say, investing or more traditional trading?

It lets you control more with your money.

If you've ever tried investing in stocks, you've likely quickly realized that you can't afford to get shares in any of the big names like Amazon or Tesla, meaning you'd have had to settle for lesser known but still profitable businesses.

However, an option for stocks is always cheaper than an equal amount of the actual stocks. An options contract for 100 shares in Amazon, for example, is always going to be much cheaper than buying those 100 shares outright. And yet, despite being much cheaper, you still get a great deal of control over those shares for a limited period of time. Pick the right time to have control, and options are simply a cheaper and more efficient way to trade stocks.

For a real life example, I've seen Tesla stocks priced at over $800 per share, yet an options contract priced at only $20 per share. Options are a way for you to play with the shares of the big names on a modest budget, potentially leading to great profits when things turn out well, all for minimal potential loss thanks to that low $20 premium.

You can swing trade more conveniently with options.

Some options traders like to glue themselves to their PC monitors day in and out for that perfect sale, devoting their whole lives to getting the best trades they can. This CAN be you, but it doesn't *have* to be. Instead, you can get options that let you check in only every few days. This makes it a great side-job, and one that you can perform from the comfort of your own home with arguably fewer hassles compared to trading and shipping physical goods.

You want flexibility that traditional investing just doesn't have.

Owning stocks directly is great for the long-term, but can be a hassle when you need to be able to quickly liquidate their value into money you can actually spend. Options meanwhile let you get trade value from stocks without tying you down with them, since you're never obligated to buy or sell any stocks if you don't want to. You simply have the *option* to do so when the market is ready to buy them off you at a good price.

It rewards active trading.

While options trading can require you to step back and just let things happen to some degree, it's to a far lesser degree than traditional stocks. If you like being more hands-on with your assets and want to be productive while doing so, options trading can feel more rewarding than investing.

Key Reasons to Rethink Trading Options, and General Disadvantages to be Aware of

Let's be frank: while anyone can trade in options, not everyone starts with the kind of composure to do so immediately. Here are some real risks to be aware of, as well as reasons why you might want to focus more on savings or passive investments before coming back to this crash course.

Options trading can be complex.

If I were writing a book on investment, I can tell you now I wouldn't need to include a glossary. For something like an investment, you just pick a company that looks like they'll be developing more and more in the long term. For options, you have more... well... options. This is great for some, but can lead to decision paralysis in others. For example, while stocks usually require only one decision to be made (invest or not?) the most basic option requires three decisions, or rather predictions (Jackson, 2021):

1. Decide (predict) whether an option's attached asset will go up or down in value
2. Decide to what degree it'll likely go up or down

3. Decide how soon or how long this change might take

Considering no one has a crystal ball in this field, that's an awful lot of predictions to make for even a basic options contract. To get around this, you'll see I'll highly recommend the KISS method:

Keep

It

Simple,

Silly!

Part of this means accepting that you'll have losses. The other part is aiming not for ultimate perfection, but rather for consistent adequacy.

So, instead of trying to win 100% of the time, you simply pick a strategy (or a few strategies) that'll let you win more often than you'll lose, letting you win out in the long term with minimal fuss. For beginners especially, I recommend starting with options that have long durations so that you don't overwhelm yourself with a high frequency of trading, especially since this is likely just your side-hustle.

The costs can add up.

Buying individual options is much cheaper than buying individual stocks. However, it's also riskier if you don't know what you're doing. Granted, you'll lose less for each individual mistake, but a lot of little mistakes can add up really quickly. Also, unlike stocks, options don't entitle you to dividends. Meaning, options don't reward you simply for holding onto them. They must be bought, sold, or traded to generate value for you.

Note that some tax laws also mean your government can charge you more when trading things you hold for less than a year, which is something you'll be doing often with options especially compared to more traditional investment.

Risks can vary.

A big mistake I see people make is the assumption that all options have the same level or even the same kind of risk. Not so. Look back to what you read on what makes options profitable. The one who writes up an option and the one who buys it both deal with very different kinds of risks, and a person who is able to manage one kind of risk might not yet be equipped to manage the other. More advanced or complex strategies also tend to carry a different kind of risk, which can be elaborated on later.

However, it's worth noting that not all assets are of equal risk either. A government bond is much less risky than a high-yield common stock for example. However, long-term investing generally doesn't have to worry much about what the market does. An option trader, however, needs to care at least a little bit about the market in order to succeed.

It can be time-consuming for some.

For a pure investment portfolio, you normally only have to check it every few months. Here, you'll be checking your options every few days. If you want to be the best of the best, you'd need to do this full time. However, it's still fully possible to profit nicely without going to such extremes of time commitment. Just be aware that, while you'll be prosperous, you likely won't be a big-name option trader. But that's okay. You'll still be good enough to get closer to where you want to be in your life as a whole.

Compared to conventional investors, you need to be more intimately aware of the company assets attached to any given option.

Now, all investors and traders need to do research. This is a given. It's a bad idea to sink money into something you know nothing about. However, because options traders need to be more intimate with the market compared to investors, it stands to reason you also need to be more familiar with the companies operating in this market. At least, the companies whose assets you wish to control via options.

For this reason, it's a good idea to go for companies whose products you use in real life, or whose mission, vision, goal, and recent activities are known to you. Both good and bad.

More on Option Flexibility

Just to end on a positive note, here are four key ways in which options grant you flexibility, especially as a buyer instead of a writer:

1. Even in the worst case scenario where your option looks like it'll be out of the money (opposite of in the money), you can still (as a buyer) recoup some of your losses by selling the contract to another investor, meaning you can ameliorate the already minimal potential losses of being an option buyer.

2. When it's in-the-money, you can typically sell it with ease to another investor for profit and not have to worry about it again, enjoying the money you've just made.

3. When you choose to exercise your option and it's a call that's in the money, you can use that call to become an investor in valuable assets at an effectively discounted price.

4. When you choose to exercise your option and it's a call that's in the money, you can buy up all the stock only to sell it all for huge profits.

So as you can see, lots of options with options! Option writers, as well as those who bought puts, also have flexibility, but generally require more advanced strategies to realize this. For instance, an option writer can choose to buy back their contract if it looks like it might get in the money for whoever bought it. This relies on whoever you sold it to agreeing to sell it back, but does greatly reduce what could otherwise be a big loss, reducing one of the biggest downsides of writing options as opposed to buying them.

Chapter 3: The Beginner's Set Up & Strategies

Now, we're almost ready to start looking at the basic strategies you can use to reach success. Before that, however, let's cover a few practical tips and tools to help you get started.

Setting Yourself Up To Trade, Step-By-Step

Choose an Option Chain and Broker

This is a matrix or rather a table that lists current available options for a given asset type in a market. It shows a list of calls, puts, their expiration dates, their strike prices, and more. They're updated in real-time, and are a great way to keep up-to-date while trading. Definitely download one now if you haven't already. This is typically done through a broker or financial services provider. Google, "Options Trading Platforms," read the reviews and feedback for the various platforms you're presented with, and you'll quickly find yourself on the right track.

It's not expected that you'll have a hard time picking a trading platform and a broker to suit your needs. However, if you're unsure, skip now to Chapter 6 to read the information on brokers there.

However, even now there are few things I recommend you look out for:

- In general, make sure that you at least check for any inactivity fees they may charge, so that you don't get punished for swing-trading by a broker who expected you to day-trade.

- If possible, pick a broker or platform that allows demo accounts. Later on, you will see why you'd want access to a demo account for trading, and it's just convenient for your demo account and your real one to be under the same broker.

- Building on that, you want your broker to have free resources to help grow your knowledge as a trader, whether that's through courses, webinars, or really good customer service/ guidance.

- Good customer service at the hours you need, via the communication channel you need (e.g. email, phone, or online media platform) is an absolute must, especially as a new trader, as the last thing you want is to feel lost and alone when you're just starting out.

- A guided tour of the option chain and/ or trading platform they use. Platforms with a user-friendly interface are good, as are ones that allow you to make or set alerts and generally allow you to do what you need to be able to do with relative ease.

- How well the broker supplies you with data, charts, and various risk/ reward analyses, all of which helps make life much easier for you, as research and information is a big part of trading options well, whether you're doing so rapidly or at a more passive/measured pace.

Pick a Strategy

As you'll see later, there're many to choose from. Make sure to start with one that's comfortable for your budget and level of risk tolerance.

Start Backtesting

Backtesting is a core fundamental part of being a successful trader. As mentioned earlier, you will have losses as an option trader, and your success will come from your ability to weather those losses until you reach the payoffs which keep your efforts profitable on average.

However, reaching those payoffs requires a level of conviction and morale that simply cannot be taken for granted. You're not a robot who can just sit there and witness loss after loss without anxiety. Nor are you a Hollywood lemming who can approach what looks like financial suicide without panic.

Backtesting as a tool is what lets you see if the strategies you wish to use are any good for the market you're working with. It can let you see if the odds are in your favor without risking any real money. Then, if your strategy is indeed good enough, you can then practice it with confidence, absorbing losses without mentally breaking so you can enjoy the sweet, sweet payoffs that come from your patience and resilience.

To successfully backtest, you'll need to do the following (Teo, 2020):

Pick a backtesting software.

MT4 or TradingView are free but slow examples of backtesting software, while something like Forex Tester has more data to work with but is a paid program. Amibroker is much more powerful than both, but is again paid and requires you to know a little bit of coding. These aren't the only backtesting softwares, so take a little time to find one that you like, and be sure to read any additional online tips on how to use it, so you get the most out of it possible.

Decide what kind of conditions are favorable for your strategy.

While we're only looking at strategies a little later, this is something good to keep in the back of your mind now. These conditions are your "trading setup," which helps determine if a trade is even worth looking at or considering. This is important as the conditions for that favor one option type, or even option strategy, won't automatically favor the next strategy or type.

Decide on your risk tolerance.

Choose, on average, how much money or what asset size is going into any single trade, or into a single kind of trade (e.g. buying multiple options in one asset type from one company is still considered a single trade for the purpose of risk tolerance).

When options trading, we always like to keep how much money we put into any single trade consistent, so this is great. We don't fluctuate wildly between trading low amounts and trading massive amounts on a single contract. We put in the same amount for each one, more or less.

So, decide now how much money you want to be putting into any single trade on average. This should be based purely on what you can comfortably afford; usually, you won't want to put any more than 1-5% of your trading account's value into any single trade.

The London Academy of Trading itself further recommends that if you lose more than 2% of your account's value in one day, then you should stop trading for that day. Likewise, if you lose more than 4% of your account's value in one week, you should stop trading for that week. This is so that your losses stay within manageable levels that your returns can still cover fairly easily. From this point onwards, I'm going to refer to these rules as *the 1-5% rule*.

Beginners should never go above those rules, ~~even~~ *especially* if they're on a winning streak. Never increase your risk tolerance just because you're winning *at the moment*. The more you put into one trade, the more likely you are to empty your trading account pretty quickly as you won't be able to sustain enough losses to make it to your profit or return months.

Decide on your time frame.

As in, how much time passes between the opening of the trade (e.g. buying a call) and closing it, (trading the call or exercising its rights). As recommended earlier, beginners will want longer time frames for each trade, such as a few weeks or even months, and will seek options with a duration to match.

Decide what market you'll be trading in.

Or markets, if you're diversifying broadly. A strategy that works well in the tech market might not be the best in textiles or agriculture. Granted, it *might* still work well, but it's incredibly irresponsible to assume so without confirmation. Always backtest for each separate market you plan to trade within.

Decide on a trade trigger.

This is like a trading setup, but more specific. A setup for a call might be, "consider making a trade when an upward trend has shown for the past few weeks in these assets," but the trigger might be, "buy the call when the value has just climbed up by X% after a dip." Don't worry about picking the perfect trigger here. Remember, we're backtesting; finding faults that we can then improve is the point of using this software.

Decide on your stop loss.

A stop loss order is another kind of trading tool that automatically closes a trade if it's skewing too out of your favor. In options trading, this would normally mean trading your options contract off at a loss in order to recoup some of what you spent, minimizing the predicted loss you would've endured had you been stubborn.

Give some thought to how you'll close or exit your trade if it's in-the-money.

Especially since options have many ways for you to get out, you'll want to test multiple exit strategies to see which works best for you on average. Plan this out beforehand so that you know what you're doing on the actual day. Otherwise, you might stress or be indecisive, which can ruin your trade.

Caveats of Backtesting

As useful as backtesting can be, it does have some things to be aware of:

- It uses historical data, which gives a good indication of how it'll perform, but to be extra sure you'll also want to use forward-testing, which is much like backtesting but it involves testing your strategy on a virtual level (no real money) with real-time market conditions. Here, you'll want to forward-test at least 100 trades to be super-sure that a winning strategy is indeed a winner.

- When is a strategy a winner? Newer traders often think a 100% win rate is what makes a winner, but this isn't necessarily true. When looking at your win rate, also look at what your strategy risks vs what it gains. For example, if your strategy involves writing puts, that's a limited gain for unlimited risk, so you'd want the win rate to be as high as possible there; each loss could be devastating.

However, if your strategy had a potential loss of up to $100, and a potential profit of up to $200, then even with a 50% win rate you're still making up to $100 profit on average. A simplified example, I know, but you get the point.

Strategies with limitless profit potential are harder to calculate properly, but for beginners try to stay above 50%, and don't feel the need to push too much further past 80%.

- Backtests, even when paired with forward tests, won't be a 100% mirror of how things will really play out. Common reasons for this are phenomena like _slippage_ or _execution errors_. Backtests act like a robot is doing the trades, but in real life it'll be a human. Decisions made out of fear, panic, or a desire to "feel better" will give you different results from what your backtest shows.

Be Aware of Market Cycles

Much like how the moon rotates around the Earth, the Earth rotates around our Sun, and our Sun spins along the axis of the Milky Way with the rest of our galaxy's stars, any market you work in will move in cycles. A cycle can last weeks, years, or even decades.

However, not all levels of cycles are relevant to everyone. For instance, a day trader will see multiple full cycles within 24 hours, whereas swing traders won't see or even need to worry about nearly so many cycles, since they're operating within a different time frame.

No matter the length, a cycle will go through four key stages (Hall, 2019):

1: Build-up or accumulation.

This is when the market has recently hit rock bottom or had a nasty tumble, but professional insiders and experienced traders have begun to put money back in, believing the worst of the storm has passed. For longer-term cycles, news articles around this market will still read as if they're calling out the doomsday of this industry. Most professionals believe that asset values will continue to decline for the moment, and may be more open to purchasing puts until things normalize.

2: Mark-up or greed.

After a period of growth and stability, the media begins to say the worst might be over. Minimum and maximum asset values on this market begin to climb higher. It's good for beginners to get in on a market early during this part of the cycle.

The end or late stage of this phase can be recognized when the volume of trades as well as the value of trades shoots up by an enormous amount. You'll also recognize the end of this stage by the fact that, while growth will continue and values continue to be high, the rate at which this growth happens will slow soon after the big initial rise.

At this point, there's huge optimism that prices and values of assets will just keep rising, but experienced traders and insiders have usually begun selling off assets long before the last late surge of the majority arrives.

3: Seller or distribution phase.

At this point, the market settles into a stable trading range that can last for many days or even months, if not more. The mass hype and hysteria around the market begins to become a little more grounded and cautious. Eventually, everyone's looking to sell their assets.

4: Mark-down or denouement.

By now, asset values have begun to plummet, with market value overall going down by up to 50%. Very few in this phase are looking to buy, and most are selling at a loss. A bad time to sell puts, especially if you're inexperienced, as your buyers will almost certainly have a reason to exercise their options. Once this 50% reduction in value has been reached however, experienced traders will be expecting the 'bottom' to be hit soon, by which point the build-up will commence once again.

Addendum: the fifth or 'politics' stage.

Not a stage per se, but something extra to be aware of; the politics of a country can have a huge effect on its markets, such as the Presidential election on US markets. Be sure to gather historical data on how recurring political events impact the markets you wish to explore.

Final Note on Market Cycles

You'll notice in the four main stages we used the words 'assets,' not 'options.' This is because these cycles don't impact options directly. However, they do directly impact the value of assets tied to your options. They also help you determine what kind of rise or drop in value you can expect from assets attached to an option. Note that these cycles aren't absolute: they're a guideline and a basepoint to help you make judgments. They are not some magical prophesying of the future, just an estimation based on past recurring evidence.

Now, Don't Start Trading Straight Away: Simulate First

Using your knowledge, put it to the test first with a trading simulator, ideally one that's closest to the market you want to work in, and see how close the results are to your backtest. This can help build your confidence further, especially if you're new, and this is important for your psychology as a trader once you have a working strategy.

After That, Open a Demo Account

A demo account is a way for you to build your skills without risking your money. It's effectively a place to practice. Much like a sports team will practice to make sure they win their match, or a musician will practice to make sure their concert touches hearts, you want to practice trading so you can act with consistency and discipline when entering and exiting your trades for real.

Next, Keep Your Head on Right, and Your Wallet Tight

You don't necessarily need a huge monthly budget to trade options, especially if it's just on a small scale with minor companies.

That said, you have likely seen that many brokers who help you make your trades require you to have a minimum amount of money that you can set aside up-front before opening your trading account. Even if you somehow work out a way to trade independently, it's useful to use those amounts as a guideline for how much money you should save up before getting into trading all on your own.

As you read earlier, execution errors are a big reason why we don't always earn as much as we predicted. You absolutely need a buffer zone, or safety net, to ensure you don't drive yourself into that state of panic which pretty proactively prompts staggering and simultaneously silly execution errors. Having a large amount of starting capital that you can set aside explicitly for trading is that buffer zone.

Next, and this cannot be emphasized enough, ***don't get greedy***. Just because the market's climbing in value doesn't mean you need to put more of your budget towards trading, or even that you should. Don't expect to know exactly where you are in any given part of a cycle at all times; you know the basic theory, but the deep sense of how a market moves or acts can only come with experience. If the modest amount you're putting in is profitable, then stick to that amount, even if you get the urge to risk more. Give the market time to show you the weird and wonderful things it can do before committing anything more than you can already consistently do.

Basic Strategies

Now, without further ado, some strategies. The married put, covered call, or even a combination of the two are all excellent choices for you to try even now, but I'd recommend at least reading the rest of this book before attempting the others.

The Debit Spread

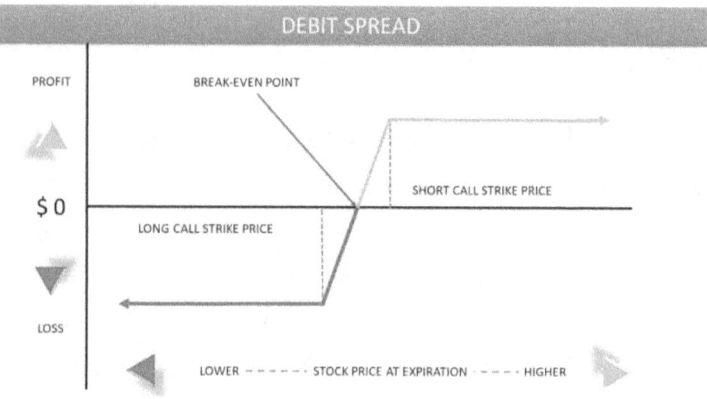

This one really is basic, and is often seen among semi-new traders who have learned the ropes. A debit spread involves two things: buying one option and selling another option.

The options must be attached to the same asset type.

For example, don't write an option on fixed income, while buying one for real estate. Keep them both attached to the same class type, so changes in the market will affect them the same way.

They must also either both be puts, or both be calls.

You cannot have one be a put and another a call. However, their strike prices or durations will differ. Calls are best if you think the market will rise, while puts are better if you think it will fall.

Finally, the option you buy must have a higher premium than the one you sell.

This means you initially seem to 'lose' when you open the trade, in the sense that you spent more money than you earned with this exchange.

However, it also means that the option you sell can be given a less favorable strike price (higher if it's a call, lower if it's a put) or duration compared to the option you bought. This means that when your option is in the money, the option you sold either won't be or will have timed out, meaning you not only get the profit/ protection from the option you bought, but also get to keep the premium from the one you sold. It's maximized gains for minimal risk.

However, it also relies on the market to change, but not too much. After all, if it rises (calls) or falls (puts) too much too quickly, then whoever you sold the cheaper option to will likely have a good opportunity to exercise its rights as well. This will dent your profits considerably, though that won't necessarily mean an outright loss.

Still, to avoid that dent, this strategy is best used when the market is relatively consistent with mild trends, and avoided when it is highly volatile.

Also, this is not to be confused with the credit spread, which tends to have a much bigger potential for risk.

The Covered Call

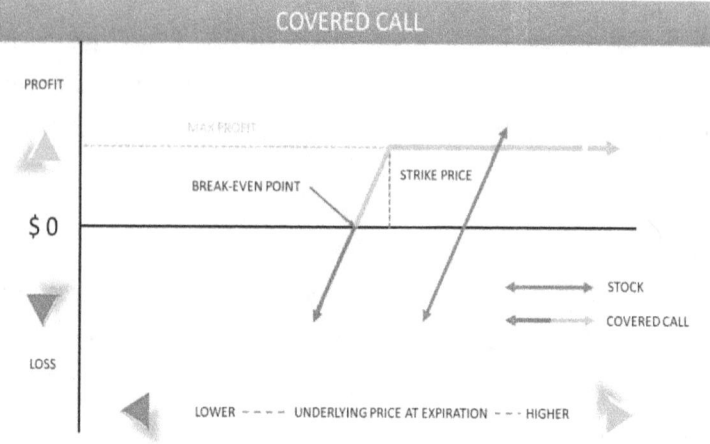

The most passive options trading strategy. If you want to earn your options income in the most hands-off way possible, this will be your go-to strategy.

To perform this strategy, you first need to buy stocks. Have at least 100 shares.

Then, sell a single call contract for every 100 shares you own. You don't want to sell contracts entitling people to more shares than you actually have.

Then, simply wait for the call contracts to expire.

This strategy is ideal for those already thinking of investing, as most of the time it simply boosts the income they get from their stocks. It works best when you believe that the value of your stocks won't rise much in the short-term.

A downside for traders, but not so much for most long-term investors, is that a covered call demands that you hold onto the stocks for the duration of the call. It also requires you to invest in stocks that, in the present, aren't likely to pay for themselves much in the short-term (though if you choose your stocks wisely, that can certainly change in the long run).

The worst case scenario here is that the stocks get bought off of you for less than they're worth, but there's no reason why you can't match the strike price to be close to what you originally paid for the stocks, ensuring overall losses are minimal.

You could even, if you buy cheap and wait for your stocks to appreciate in value a bit first, set the strike price to be above what you paid for the stocks originally, ensuring you profit either way. This can be done if you manage to buy stocks early in an accumulation stage of your market's cycle, then write and sell the call options on them late in that same market's greed stage.

Just remember that higher strike prices on calls tend to mean lower premiums.

The Naked Call

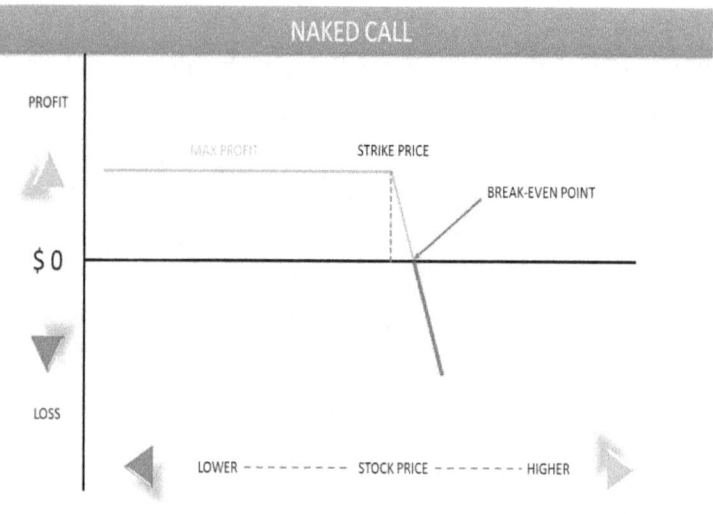

This is much like a covered call, except you do not actually own whatever you wrote the call for. This isn't a basic strategy so much as an early cautionary note. Some particularly aggressive, well-versed, or stupidly rich traders can get away with this, but I wouldn't recommend this even as an advanced strategy.

Many brokers also outright ban this practice for most of their traders, and for good reason.

The profit is limited to the premium you get, while the losses are potentially limitless as you'll be obligated to relinquish money for stocks whose prices may have shot through the roof, with no way to ameliorate this circumstance. Sure, you can have a "just in case" budget set aside beforehand, but at that point you're honestly better off spending that to own the darn stocks.

Naked calls are free money while they work... and an absolute nightmare when they don't.

The Long Call

A fancy name for something simple, this 'strategy' is just buying a call that you expect to become profitable before it expires. Don't feel intimidated if you see this term thrown about! _Long_ (synonymous with 'bullish') is just jargon for something you expect to gain in value.

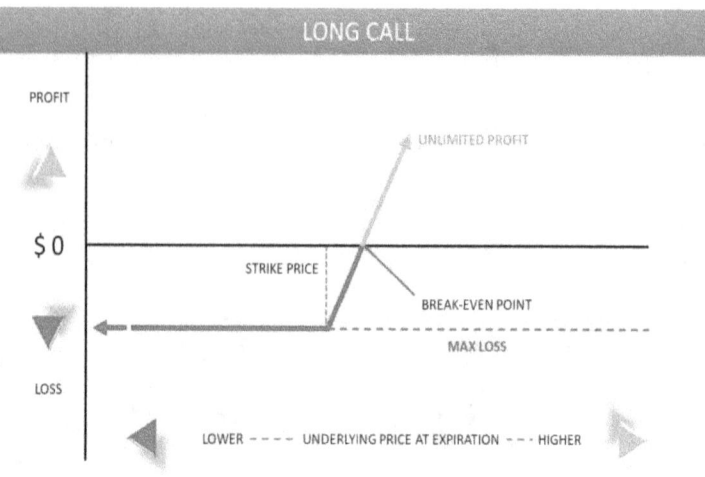

The Protected Put

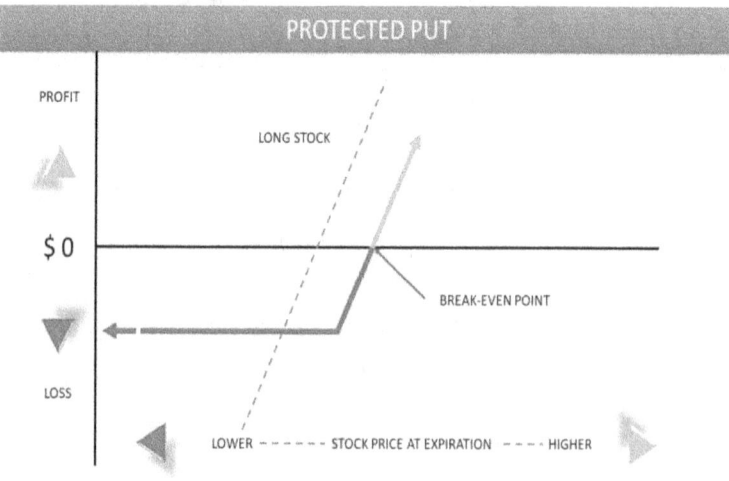

A formal name for something you already know: this is the strategy we mentioned earlier when an investor buys puts to effectively 'insure' their stocks. Requires you to buy stocks for the purpose of earning value through trades, while the puts are there as a "just in case" measure to limit risks of downturn.

Chapter 4: Tools of the Trade

While we've already touched on some basic tools, like the minimum mindset needed to reach for financial freedom, as well as what to bear in mind while backtesting, here we'll explore more tools to help you take your trading to the next level.

The Framework For Your Tools

All the tools I offer and the advice I give tries to tie into a trading framework. Namely, the four pillars of trading as recommended by the London Academy of Trading (LAT Staff, 2020).

These pillars, in order, are:

- *Trading psychology.*

  This is the biggest one, as a poor understanding of trading psychology is why so many traders end up losing more than they earn. The main objectives of trading psychology revolve around staying calm, and avoiding decisions made based on greed (excessive optimism) or fear (excessive pessimism). Any advice around maintaining a clear head and staying logical can be attributed to trading psychology.

- *Risk management.*

  Another big one, and is the pillar our 1-5% rule came from (see Glossary for a reminder if needed). This pillar focuses on conserving your capital, putting only limited amounts of money into trade at once so as to protect yourself from unexpected downturns. Risk management is the key to trading with small amounts of money, as it lets you stretch and preserve it long enough to start growing and seeing returns. Risk management naturally has a lot of overlap with trading psychology, since it involves beating back greed.

- *Fundamental analysis.*

  This involves gathering information on inflation rates, gross domestic product, employment rates, interest rates, and more. You'd typically gather this information according to the company whose stock you're going to be buying a lot of options on, as that'll tell you which country's data to use for the information types listed above. This form of analysis can also involve a specific company's news articles, balance sheets, and financial statements in order to see how they fare compared to their competition.

- *Technical analysis.*

  This pillar is centered on examining a market's data directly, rather than the data of an underlying company or the country it's based in. The trade prices and volume of trades you see when looking at a chart for a market's performance data can offer valuable insights into what part of the cycle it is currently in.

The tools below do not conform neatly to any one pillar, but rather use a blend of ideas derived from them. Without further ado, let us examine and internalize them.

Tool #1: Awareness of Your Own Mortality

A tad morbid, yes, but internalize now that you are not a god. You are mortal. The laws of physics and probability do not bend to serve you, nor are you invincible, even if you're still young and at an age where you naturally feel like you can take on the world.

Building on that, you need to be aware that you're not omniscient either. At several points before this we touched on how it's a bad idea to assume you know what a market will do, especially without testing. The reason for this is simple:

You Don't Know What You Don't Know

There's always more for you to learn before you can approach a complete perspective. This book is here to give you a baseline, or to add a bit to existing knowledge, but it shouldn't be taken as your only resource if you wish to keep improving and upping your game. You will want to make friends with people who have experience in finance. Long-term relationships with those older and wiser than you can turn into a great source of mentorship later. I say long-term, because this is your money you're working with here. You want to be sure you're taking advice from someone you can trust.

Peer-reviewed forums are a good place to start, though don't get too glued to any single one, as just like how no one person can know everything, likewise no single group will be without blindspots.

Even I still have a lot to learn! For this reason, don't hesitate to leave me a review later, especially if you've enjoyed the book. Feedback is always valuable. Never stop seeking it.

Remember to Expand Your Knowledge With Technical and Fundamental Analysis

It isn't difficult to get the basics of it down. Technical data can be gathered pretty easily by looking at the historic returns, prices, and trade quantities of a stock or option over the years. From there, your understanding of market cycles can give you a better idea of what a stock or option might do in the near future. Backtesting, due to its reliance on historical data, is arguably a form of technical analysis.

Fundamental analysis, meanwhile, focuses on paying close attention to the trends of a corporation and its country overall. It doesn't necessarily care what stage of the market cycle your market might be, but rather it can forewarn you of special or unexpected shifts relative to your market's performance. The best way to use fundamental analysis, especially if you only hold your options for a few days at a time, is to know in advance when data such as unemployment rates, industry outputs or more will be released, as you'll then be able to see it potentially before many other traders are even aware of it. This can be helpful if you know the data released has implications for your market.

Use both forms of analysis together as much as you can, as technical analysis can tell you how a market is generally, while fundamental analysis can tell you to what degree a specific company's assets will follow a market's overall trend.

Not all companies are impacted the same way in each phase of a market cycle, after all, and fundamental analysis can help spot when a company's assets may behave anomalously compared to the market as a whole.

Note that while some advanced tips will be given on analysis in Chapter 6, it's only a taste of the total pool of knowledge out there. Never stop learning.

Is It Possible to Know Too Much?

Granted, if you're trading options as a side-hustle, you may reach a point where you feel like it just isn't worth it to do more research. Once you take in enough theory, you may be comfortable learning the rest through experience. If you're able to get by and profit nicely, then fair enough, though more research never hurts.

However, if you ever wish to devote more time to trading, or even do so full-time, accept that your learning will never end, and that it is impossible to know too much about the field you're working in.

In these cases, you'll want to learn as much as you humanly can without exhausting yourself or distracting yourself from your values. This is because the strategies you learn about now aren't the only strategies out there, and new ones will be tested and conceived of.

Learning about these new ways of trading options will let you spot whether or not you're going into a deal that'll favor you, as you'll have an easier time seeing what your fellow trader in this deal is trying to do.

Case Studies on the Lie of Invincibility

These hypotheticals are based on real experiences that occurred while options trading.

Fred's Story

Fred decides to open his trading account with a broker, who asks him to have $3000 available to open his account. Fred gradually saves that amount, and finally opens.

He now has $3000 to spend however he wishes on options trades.

Now, you might remember earlier that one shouldn't spend more than 1-5% of their account on any single trade. Fred knows this guideline, and then modestly buys a call for a total of $60. Happily, he's still early in his market's greed stage, so this call works out for him.

Let's say he earns a profit of $30 in this case. Now, he does it again, taking out the exact same type of call again with the same duration, premium, and strike price. Again, he wins, but this time he gets a profit of $45 from the same. More than last time. Nice.

So he does it again. This time he earns $60 worth of profit. This means he spent $60 and got $120 back. Now, Fred begins to feel really lucky.

Round four. He chooses to take out multiple options on the *exact same asset*, with the *same duration*, and the *same strike price*. So, effectively, it's still one trade, because all of it wins and loses based on exactly the same conditions.

This time, he's spent a total of around $180 as he buys three options. Sadly, these were bought near the end of the greed stage, and a dip in the market means all three options turn out worthless. Meaning, he earned $30, then $45, then $60... only to lose $180, for a net loss of $45.

So, what could've been a good few weeks or months of trading has effectively lost him more than he earned. But what if he stayed consistent?

What if he only spent the same $60 he always spent, instead of spending that $180?

Then, even though he would've lost that one option in round four, he still would've profited overall. He'd have earned $30, then $45, then $60... only to lose $60. No biggy, he'd have still effectively won $75.

The probability of options trading means you have to lose at some point. The nature of options trading means there's a winner and a loser, as the success of the option writer and the success of the option buyer are normally antagonistic to one another.

There wouldn't be a market for this kind of commerce if most people won all the time. However, if they know what they're doing, everyone can still net out an overall profit *most* of the time.

This is why I keep saying you should keep the money you put in consistent. That way, when you occasionally lose, it won't hurt much compared to all the wins you've already had, or the wins your backtesting says you'll soon have. Speaking of which...

Freda's Story

Now we're going to look at someone else, who we'll call Freda. Freda is incredibly smart. She found a winning strategy that she's back-tested and front-tested all day long in December. It has an 80% chance of working. In January, she opens her account with the same broker Fred did, with $3000 for trading sitting in her account too.

Because her strategy has such a high success chance, she thinks, "Well, why trade small? Let's go big right away."

So she spends $750 on premiums for a single trade (or a single group of trades tied to the same kind of asset). Surprisingly, she loses. Her options expire worthless, and she is down $750. What happened? Unbeknownst to her, she just entered the market at a time of heavy distribution.

But she thinks to herself, "An 80% success rate means I'll only lose once every five times, so it should be okay to just do this again."

So she does. Another $750 in. Again, her options expire worthless. So, stressing out, she immediately puts $1500 to try to feel better, thinking this is the big one. After all, what are the odds of an 80% success strategy failing three times in a row?

It fails again. Her account, now empty, is forced to close, and she has just lost $3000.

Later, she goes back to her backtesting. She feels frustrated, not understanding what happened. Then she sees it. That 80% success rate? That was an average for over the course of a full market cycle. And she came in at the worst part of the cycle for her strategy.

But she couldn't have known. However, if she'd moderated her spending on trades, she'd have been able to withstand the losses easily while she got a feel for the ebb and flow of the market she was entering.

If she only spent $30 or $60 on any one kind of option at a time, then she could've had a dozen losses and still been fine, with a much better chance of having her account survive into the good part of the market cycle, where that 80% success rate strategy would have proven its worth four times over for every loss she had to endure in the meantime.

Tool #2: Understand the Value of Time

"Time is money" is a pretty cliche phrase at this point, but it's not without its merits.

Time Value of Money

This is a fundamental financial concept that can help take your options trading to the next level.

The time value of money (TVM) states that any money you might own now is more valuable than any equal amount of money you might own in the future.

Usually, this is due to inflation or price rises in relation to spending power. For instance, one reason money is valuable is due to its ability to buy food. Let's say a loaf of bread costs $8, and you have $16 to spend on bread each week. Right now, that's two loaves of bread each week.

But what if the price of bread later rises to $9 thanks to inflation? Well, now you can only buy one loaf of bread, and will need to add more money to your bread budget before you can afford another. The spending power of your money has gone down.

And so it goes. I often advise beginners to pick options that have durations measured in weeks or months, but it's important to be cognizant of the time value of money while holding these options. In the US, most goods go up by an average of 1-3% in price over the course of a year. Some countries, and some years, see a larger increase.

Considering most options contracts run for less than a year, the effect of inflation on your earnings is usually negligible, but do bear this in mind. It effectively means that "breaking even" on an option you bought is still a loss, albeit a slight one.

It also means you don't want your option to be only barely in the money before you exercise it. Unless you have strong reasons to believe the option will quickly go out of your favor if you wait, rather wait until the profit you get is at least 1-3% higher than what it needs to be to be considered "in the money."

Usually, the profit you get will exceed that naturally, but knowing the current rate of inflation can help decide whether to exercise your option immediately or give it a minute.

Time Value for Options

Of course, for options traders a more noticeable effect of time would be all the market changes that happen within any given period.

Here, the time value of an option can drastically alter the premium you can buy or sell it for. If you originally bought an option that you're now looking to trade, this option's time value can affect how good a price you can expect, as mentioned earlier.

However, there's a little more to it than that.

For instance, time value has the biggest impact on options that are *at the money* (like in-the-money, but leads to breaking even instead of profit if exercised). When an option is so close to being in the money, then all that really matters is how much time it has left to change. This means if you own an option that's at the money, and aren't sure you want to exercise it, then you'll want to sell it as soon as possible instead, as your likelihood of getting a higher premium for it than you paid will only go down with every second that passes.

However, if an option is really far away from being in-the-money, its duration will have less of an impact. This is because there'll be doubts as to whether it'll ever *be* in the money, usually because the strike price is so far from the current price that it's believed there's no way the market will cause a fast enough growth or decline to profit off the option. This is why, when writing options, you can give it the longest duration on Earth but you'll still battle selling it for a good premium if it's too unfavorable.

However, if you have an option that's already in-the-money, and you don't wish to exercise it for whatever reason, it's worth noting that people tend to care less about duration in these cases too. Duration still has an impact, but most people are going to want to cash in on the option as soon as they can, with remaining duration not being as relevant. Of course, that doesn't mean duration has *no* impact, only that you don't need to rush if you want to sell the option like you would for one that's at-the-money. This scenario of selling an in-the-money option is most often seen with European options, where it's possible to see a contract go into the money and then out of the money before you reach the date to exercise it.

Employing the Greeks

In the last chapter, we threw around a few Deltas, Gammas, and so forth. These are what options traders collectively refer to as The Greeks, as they derive from the Greek alphabet. Each Greek — Delta, Gamma, Theta, and Vega — symbolizes *change*.

Specifically, *change* over *time*.

Respectively, changes in asset price (Delta), the speed at which asset price changes (Gamma), the impact of changes in duration (Theta, e.g. how much premium value is lost in a day), and changes in market volatility (Vega).

Delta, Theta, and Vega all directly impact the premium you can trade an options contract for, whether you're the writer or whether you're a buyer who wants to now sell or pass the option onto someone else. Gamma, meanwhile, only impacts Delta.

Now, earlier I mentioned that these are essentially algebraic symbols, used to calculate the kind of risks you can expect over a certain period of time. However, you may have wondered, 'How?'

We're not going to go into too much depth here, but note that these calculations aren't intended to be done mentally, or by hand. Instead, you'll use an online calculator, or download software especially designed to calculate the greeks for you. A common way of doing this is with a standard *Black & Scholes* Options Calculator.

To use this calculator, you'll be asked to input a variety of information, namely:

- A spot price (or simply 'price'). This is just the price at which the asset attached to your option is currently trading.

- Interest. For this, insert the market economy's prevailing risk-free interest rate. In the US this is the Treasury Note rate. Other countries might call this a Treasury Bill rate instead.

- Dividends. If the shares attached to your option are going to have their dividends paid before your option expires, simply plug in the total expected dividend amount for each share each time the dividends get paid out between now and option expiry. If no dividend payouts are happening before expiry, simply put a zero in instead.

- Days until expiry. Exactly what it says on the tin, with hours rounded up to the nearest day. If today's the 24th of Dec and your option expires on the 25th, you'd have exactly 1 calendar day until expiry right up until the date officially changes to the 25th.

- Volatility. Here, simply plug in the relevant IV (Implied Volatility) value from your Options Chain.

Quick tips on using the Greek Values you get:

1. The closer to 1 your Delta value is, the more in-the-money your option is IF IT IS A CALL. Likewise, the closer to -1 it is for a put, the better for you. This value will shift a bit as the expiration date draws nearer, so you can recheck your option's delta value every day if you like to help decide if it's worth holding on. A value of 0.50 is "at the money" for a call, while -0.50 is likewise for a put.

2. Gamma is also between -1 and 1, and tells you by how much Delta is likely to change soon. If Gamma is 0.15, then Delta is going to likely raise by about 0.15 soon.

3. Your Theta value tells you how much premium value will be lost each day as expiration draws nearer... assuming all other Greek values remain constant.

4. The higher Vega is, the more premium value a call or put is entitled to. If Vega is below the market average, consider using a buying strategy (since your losses from premiums will be lower). If Vega is above market average, use a selling strategy (since you earn more relative to your potential losses).

5. If you're using a *Black & Scholes* calculator, you'll also be given the Premium value for calls and puts around the option you're examining. This can help you see how much you may be overpaying or underselling your current options.

Tool #3: Your Brain (Your Source of Trading Discipline)

An underrated tool, it happens to be what makes literally every single decision you take in life, including your financial ones. So, it's important to examine it.

As patience, mindset, and simple, clear strategy are what helps you succeed, it pays to focus some time and energy on choices and activities that boost these attributes.

Know When to Log Off

Unless you're day trading, you don't exactly need to be glued to your screen. For whatever market you're working with, make sure you know their most active hours where watching and trading is a worthwhile use of your time. This can usually be done with a quick Google search.

However, no matter what their times are, always aim to shut your computer down and finish the day's trading about 40 minutes before you plan to sleep. This is because computer screens stimulate the brain into staying awake longer than it should. This leads to fatigue, which slows down your nervous system. The net effect, over time, can be comparable to being drunk.

Now, would you dare to trade while drunk? Of course not! So, bear this knowledge in mind and keep to it consistently; there's no such thing as "sleep debt," only sleep duration and sleep consistency, with consistency being the most important component for proper mental functioning.

Keep a Flask Handy

While an open-topped cup isn't advised, a sealed flask of water is a good thing to keep by your workstation. This is because your brain mostly consists of water, which it needs to function optimally. Your heart, likewise, is also mostly water, which it needs to pump oxygen efficiently around your body. This oxygen, again, is needed by your brain to think properly. If you're experiencing brain fog, get some water.

Coffee or tea can be great about an hour before and an hour after lunch due to its stimulating effects, but it won't hydrate you like water does. No matter what other soft drinks you might be packing, always bring plenty of water.

Find Slow-Burning Snacks

A packet of chips or a hamburger might be tempting as a snack while you're sitting at your trade screen, but make sure whatever you're having is slow-burning, or low-GI. This is so you avoid the energy slumps and distracting cravings of high-GI eating. Low-GI keeps your energy levels more consistent, more predictable, and overall easier to work with. Cheese, yogurt, brown bread, and baked beans are all great choices, but not your only ones. Sites like Healthline have great lists of brain-food to help fuel your decision-making.

Keep Yourself Busy with Something

Not all your trading time needs to be spent trading, but sitting still and doing nothing can feel frustratingly boring and lead to emotional meddling.

So, if you're new and just starting on getting your system together, keeping yourself busy might mean spending some of your trading time watching YouTube videos on Options Trading, specifically on topics such as how to exit trades. Or maybe you want to see someone else's perspective on a topic that's already been covered here.

However, once you have a system that works, then while you should certainly keep learning, don't be afraid to alternate this with activities that relax you and help you feel better. Speaking of which...

Have Something on Hand to Help You Feel Better

This can be a stress ball, a doodle pad, a treadmill, a favorite book, or something else. It could even be an exercise mat where you do jumping jacks, or it can be a street nearby where you can go for a walk and cool off. It doesn't really matter what it is, only that it boosts your mood without costing much money.

This is essential as there will be times where you feel a little stressed out in your trading, and as a knee-jerk response you'll begin taking riskier trading decisions in order to feel in control. Because taking action makes us feel in control, right?

But in trading, taking the wrong action will only hurt you. It doesn't matter if it makes you feel better or not in the moment. And you're much more likely to take a wrong action when you're in fight-or-flight mode, making decisions with your sabertooth tiger-evading caveman brain instead of your more logical, trader's brain.

So, have some item or activity nearby that isn't trading-related, so when your brain is screaming, "DO SOMETHING TO FEEL BETTER," you won't feel instantly compelled to do something that'll torpedo your trading account.

Acting out of panic when making any trading decision never works. It only makes you feel better... until the fruits of that decision come forward. Then you'll feel much worse. Always do something else to alleviate your panic instead before getting back into trading.

Practice Mindfulness With Journaling

This is pretty common self-help advice, but in the context of options trading what I mean is you should have a notebook somewhere to write down the thought processes you have around the trades you make. Explain to yourself why you're doing what you're doing. This not only helps you feel more clear-headed in the moment, but it also gives you something to review later, where you can see what topics you can benefit from learning more about, or what thoughts holding you back should be double-checked just in case they're incorrect. It can take up to two years to learn how to trade options like a true pro, so writing down your thoughts can be a great way to stimulate that growth process.

Practice Trading Mindfulness With Breathing

Breathing can be done anywhere, no matter what you have at hand, so breathing with intention for mindfulness can be a great technique to have. You can do this before you open your trade screen, while you're still at peace, but you should certainly do this if you notice you're not at ease and can't shake that anxiety off.

To do this, simply seat yourself comfortably (or stand if you don't mind the strain) and let your body slowly relax, releasing each muscle from head to toe, letting that tension pass out. If your jaw is clenched, unclench it. If your shoulders are raised, lower them. If your feet are tapping, still them. Then, clear your mind and focus on your breath.

How do we focus on something like our breath? Simply by being aware of it. Do not try to control it. It's important to teach your brain that just because it notices something doesn't mean it has to meddle with it. This is essential for good trading.

You'll see loads of new and interesting trading schemes and ideas, there's just no way to try them all. Some might help, many might actually interfere with your current setup and detract from your strategy. So center yourself and teach your brain now that it doesn't have to chase after the shiny or novel all the time. Sometimes it's okay to just relax and let the process happen. If you notice your mind wandering, don't be harsh with yourself.

The act of noticing your mental wandering is a sign that your mindfulness is increasing. Simply bring your focus back to your breath in that case, and relax.

When you return to your world of trading, you can try to extrapolate this to your movements as a trader. When you notice yourself browsing news or information that doesn't make you feel better, and isn't relevant to your current trading system, then gently bring yourself back into focus on information that will help your system instead.

Treat Your Mind as a Muscle

Don't expect yourself to have perfect emotional resilience or ideal risk tolerance right out of the gate. These are muscles that need to be built, and it's all connected to your sense of experience with trading overall. A muscle grows from exertion, but try to stretch it too far too quickly, and it'll snap.

If you don't know your risk tolerance, or if you know you have a tendency to freak out while trading due to past experience, focus on low-risk over high-profit.

This is especially true if options trading is just your side-hustle, in which case you can't go wrong from starting with less profitable, but more manageable options. Starting your trading career by staking small amounts of your own money is key. You might think starting out with large amounts of borrowed money (or someone else's money in general) might make you feel better, but I've found most people actually stress out more when handling huge amounts of a firm's money instead of any amount of their own.

No one likes to think they'll make a mess-up that'll lose thousands. So, when it comes to risk, start small, and push that boundary gradually.

Tool #4: A Healthy Dose of Caution

Simply put, the market does whatever the heck it wants to. Backtesting and cycle awareness can help you predict what is most likely to happen, but as stated earlier NO ONE has true clairvoyance into the future. We're always moving blind, we just assume we know where everything is thanks to historical data. Which works out until something moves in a way that it hasn't before.

You may be tempted to fight this and, indeed, being as knowledgeable as you can is a good way to fight this. Forward-testing and probability calculation are great methods of echolocation, giving you a clearer idea of where things are.

What isn't a good way is through trying to outright control the market, or scheming to beat it through constant changes and overly-elaborate moves. This will only generate stress for you, and not necessarily earn you that much more in terms of profit, let alone emotional or time value.

If your strategy showed itself pulling an annual profit in its backtest, or at least showed itself pulling a net profit for whatever period of time you plan to trade during the year, then you're in a good space. Stick to your strategy in these cases.

However, don't ever enter a trade optimistically. Don't assume you'll gain the maximum profit possible, or that you'll get your predicted wins in the months that you want them to be in. Optimism-based decision-making can be just as bad as fear-based decision-making in options trading.

This profession is one of the most rational and logical there is; facts, as precious as they are, must always be taken over hype or speculation.

Especially considering, as our cycle awareness section shows, hype outlets like the news tend to be a little bit off when it comes to what the market is actually doing.

Granted they can be useful indicators, but that doesn't mean they should be taken at face value; just look at the typical build-up phase in a typical market cycle. The news often says the market is in a really bad place, when in fact it's actually already on the up.

Knowing just *how* off a news outlet is in any given market is, again, something that can only be gained through time and experience, further reinforcing why you should be cautious and patient with your trades. Smaller trades effectively give you more time to learn.

Chapter 5: Here Are Some Common Pitfalls — Dodge 'Em

You've taken in quite a lot of information so far around basic strategies, principles, and ways to keep your mind tradeworthy and resilient. Along the way, you'll notice we touched on a few potential pitfalls already, but here is where we examine some of the biggest or most common ones, so that you can drill into yourself the knowledge needed to learn from key mistakes before you even make them.

Or, if you're already making them, to let them go.

Top Trader Mistakes

Not Paying Attention to the Expiration Date on an Option

Now, it's rare for someone to ignore this date completely, but when the expiry is weeks or months away, some amateur traders make the mistake of not writing it down or putting it in their calendar. Make sure you have reminders for the durations on all your active trades, especially if you don't check in on your options directly that much.

Not Paying Attention to the Option Type

A similar mistake is not checking whether an option is American or European. Remember that European calls and puts will be marked with 'CE' and 'PE' respectively, while American ones will be marked with 'CA' or 'PA' instead. If a contract has none of those markings, consult your financial services provider to double-check it, though in these cases you'd have likely stumbled upon an exotic options contract, which I wouldn't recommend for anyone outside the most experienced and resilient traders.

Not Factoring Duration into Your Strategy

A long duration demands a higher premium, but in many cases a shorter one would've been just fine. Examine market trends (especially trading volumes and prices) to estimate where the market is in its cycle, then use that knowledge to more accurately estimate how long it'd take for an asset to shift a certain amount. Then, you won't be so reliant on long durations with American contracts to profit, saving yourself costs on premiums. Even if you prefer long-duration options, knowing these trends will still help you get your timing right and save on costs that way.

Not Árchiving Your Trades

Building on the above, it helps to record your trades not only to act as reminders, but also to act as past data. This is, in effect, your own personal bank of historical data that you build up and add to over time. Having a neat, easy-to-read trade history can help you a great deal as an extra information source when trying a new trade.

Ignoring the 1-5% Rule

Fred and Freda (especially Freda) have already covered why this is a bad idea, especially for beginners, but it really can't be stressed enough. This applies not just to when you start out, but also to when you're consistently growing and succeeding overall. Even as your trading account grows, keep the money you're putting into any one trade consistent, with only very gradual growth, seldom (if ever) exceeding 1-5% of your account's total.

You absolutely need to moderate yourself in this way, because while we can use backtesting and probability to gauge risk, at the end of the day the market does whatever the heck it wants. It lives and breathes according to the actions of millions of humans, and will behave oddly if the majority of humans thus decide to do something unusual, or if a far-reaching event causes them to behave differently. You need to keep how much you're putting into any one trade low, so that you keep potential losses low, so that you can have the time needed to see just what a market can do to your strategy.

This time is necessary for you to be able to decide what you can do better next time, rather than rushing to act immediately in a fear-based panic.

Where Should You Fall Between 1-5%?

Building on the above, you should choose where you fall within the 1-5% scale according to how much you can comfortably lose in a single trade. You want the size of your trades to be large enough to feel meaningful when you win, but not so large that you stay up at night stressing over whether or not it'll go through. The sleep loss will impact your performance, so if starting on the lower end is what you need for peace of mind, start there. You can always slowly increase from there later.

Getting Impatient

You don't need to be rushing to make trades every second of every day. Trades aren't inherently good or bad. They're just an opportunity to profit if the market is in your favor, or lose if it is not. Don't accumulate options just so you can say you have them. Rather, pick and choose those that look like they'll be best for you based on your strategy and what you believe the market will most likely do within the relevant timeframe.

Even with a trading setup, you've only narrowed your options down to the ones worth considering for your strategy, but not every option worth considering is worth taking. If you are feeling really unsure about a potential option, and that feeling is backed by probability and current trends, then rather look at it again tomorrow (the market might move in a direction that makes it more favorable) or forget about it and bring your attention to the next potential option.

Forming an Unhealthy Attachment With Complexity

Remember KISS.

Keep

It

Simple,

Silly!

Some traders develop a powerful attachment to complexity, but this isn't necessarily good. Options can already be quite complex compared to simply trading assets, so we don't want to add onto that needlessly.

To avoid making things overly complex, it helps to keep your trading plan succinct and well-defined. This means spending a little time with your plan. Some people shy away from spending time on trading plans, thinking that planning equates to complexity, but this is not necessarily so. A budget isn't complex, for instance, but it's still a plan that makes life much easier for its user.

Minutes of preparation can ultimately save you hours of stress and this applies not just to budgets, or even just to your trading plan, but also to the art of planning overall.

Once you know how much you're willing to put into a single trade, and once you've done enough research and analysis to find good opportunities in the market you're working with, you can finalize your plan by solidly defining two major trading points:

- How will you get into the trades you want?
- How will you get out of them?

Getting in is pretty easy, and will depend on your strategy. For instance, you'd get into a spread by buying a call and a put at the same time, under the conditions we discussed for spreads earlier.

Now, as for getting out, you need to ask:

- How will I get out if the trade is in-the-money?
- How will I get out if the trade is going bad and I need to cut my losses?

Normally, you'll answer the former with a Take-Profit order, and the latter with a Stop-Loss order. Usually you'll be able to set the duration of such orders too, so you can decide when you want the stop-loss to be active.

For instance, you might only set a Stop-Loss order on your trade when you notice a consistent downward trend, or when you're in the last few days of your option's duration. This is because you wouldn't want a short-term fluctuation to activate your option's Stop-Loss order and cause a frustrating loss when you know that there was still plenty of time for the option to bounce back.

However, that might be seen as a bit complex. To simplify, you can instead spend a few minutes researching what the usual daily price fluctuations are for your market, then simply set the stop-loss to activate if the fluctuation of your option exceeds that. This way, you can simply initiate the stop-loss and leave it.

No matter how you choose to go about entering and exiting trades, however, taking a bit of time to think about how you'll do it, in the simplest way you can, will allow you to capitalize on opportunities quickly, rather than floundering with an in-the-money option because you're unsure how to get out of it.

Addendum: When You're An Option Writer...

Always have some idea how you'll fulfill your end of the deal if whoever you wrote the option for chooses to exercise it. This is especially true if writing/ selling an option is only one part of your strategy. If that written option gets used, how will that affect the rest of your strategy?

Overobsessing With Profit

This may seem counter-intuitive, but bear with me. Profit is a noble goal, but greed can be a deceptive lure. I've seen examples where a fellow trader had a call that was well in-the-money, but believed it'd rise just that bit higher before expiry.

It took a sharp dip the day before expiration, and he was forced to sell his call off at a loss.

If you have a call that's comfortably in-the-money, and don't have much duration left, rather exercise it early, or even sell it to someone else for your profit. Obviously, you'd want to set a minimum target profit to make options trading worthwhile (e.g. beating inflation and making the time spent feel worthwhile), but there's little reason to go over that aside from greed. Greed is an emotional state of being, not a logical one, so consider carefully whether you're truly being wise or cautious to hold onto an in-the-money option just that little bit longer, or whether you're just being greedy.

This advice is essential if you ever choose to become an options writer. Many newer writers like to write a call or a put for someone, then leave it to tick out, hoping the option will never be exercised. While it's true that most options do go unexercised, it's often wiser to buy back the options you write when circumstances have made their premiums really, really cheap.

For instance, say you wrote an option with a premium worth $100 in total. The market does something that didn't favor whoever bought your option, and now it's just worth $20 in premium. You already have your $100, so you could choose to let their option expire worthless.

However, you could instead offer to buy the option back for that $20. You'd still have made $80 in profit. You'd have still won. You'd have just decided to tie up a loose end early in exchange for a little less profit. It's my recommendation that you buy back any option you write once it's way out-the-money, especially if you know it's only out-the-money due to a temporary dip.

This does reduce the profit you get per written option, but can also help you sidestep many of the normal losses associated with writing options entirely.

Overall, there is always a point where the risk associated with trying to eke out that little extra profit just isn't worth it. Learn to accept slightly lower profits when it means significantly less risk.

Forgetting That You're Working With People

You only really see numbers on screen most of the time, so it can be easy to forget that these numbers are made by people making trades just like you are now. It's imperative to note that, people being people, strange decisions will occasionally occur. For instance, maybe you decide to do a debit spread, and things seem to be working in your favor... except the person holding the option you wrote might be a total newbie this time, and exercise it way too early, netting themselves a loss.

Netting themselves a loss, while also potentially interfering with your strategy. This comes back to keeping things simple, and planning in advance how you'll handle your trades being entered and exited so you don't have to flounder on the day it happens. People will make silly mistakes. In some cases, these mistakes might not only cost them, but also you to a degree.

When entering a trade that involves writing an option for someone else, take a moment to consider what it'd mean for you if they were being very silly and exercised it way too early. It helps to be sure in advance whether such an event will help or hurt you.

Advance notice improves your chances of remaining confident, resilient, and in control when things go awry, allowing you to continue working and thinking logically rather than being put on the defensive in fight-or-flight mode.

Becoming Inflexible

It's not uncommon for traders to become inflexible to some degree. This is largely due to all the recommendations to keep growth slow and gradual, and to stick to your working strategies no matter what.

But if your accumulated experience, along with sufficient backtesting, forward-testing and probability calculation tells you that an alteration to your current strategy would favor you, then by all means make that alteration. Add and mix in different strategies once you have valid reasons to believe they work, and once you can do so in a relatively simple manner.

Why Do Some Traders Become Inflexible?

The axiom that you should stick to your strategies no matter what is only there to prevent you from making alterations based on *emotional thinking*.

However, this isn't always communicated clearly from mentor to trainee, leading to many new traders thinking they should never deviate from a working strategy ever.

That said, there's a huge difference between deviating because the data and research overwhelmingly support doing so, versus deviating because you guess or feel it might lead to better results. The problem is many new traders skimp out on tests and research, leading to *so many people changing their strategies according to what they're feeling or speculating rather than any real logic.*

In one notable case, new options traders being inducted into a firm would alter the strategies they were given based on guesses and feelings even when they were explicitly told they'd be permanently hired or promptly fired based on how closely they stuck to the strategy they were given, rather than how successful they immediately were with it.

They were also explicitly told how much profit they make (or even how many losses they incur!) with the strategy won't matter for them career-wise; not during this induction. Against all logic, almost all of them wouldn't stop meddling with the strategy they were given anyways. This is because of anxiety leading to emotional, fear-based meddling.

As a result, a lot of mentors become perhaps a little overzealous in making their trainees stick to a preset plan. This ensures the trainee has discipline and doesn't wreck themselves with their own panic, but as implied earlier it can stifle them if they don't realize why their mentor had them do this.

It's not that you aren't allowed to be flexible, but rather that you should ground your flexibility in truth and knowledge.

Making changes on a whim just because you feel like it isn't 'flexibility.' It's risk or, to put it less kindly, insanity.

Assuming You'll Always be Cool and Collected

If you're already feeling composed and in control, don't take it for granted. Remember, this emotional resilience is a muscle, and muscles need to be fed and exercised to remain strong. By all means, stick to high-duration trades that you only need to check once in a while, but always take the steps needed to assure yourself that you know how you're getting into the trade, and that when the day comes you'll know how to get out.

At the very least, keep your sleep and hydration levels on par. In the same way you shouldn't massively raise the money you sink into trades just because you're winning, you shouldn't use a winning streak as an excuse to neglect your planning and self-support either.

Diversifying Like You're Trading or Investing in Stock

While you might be trading or investing in stock directly, note that _diversification_ works a little differently with options.

With investing, the main thing to keep diverse in order to be effectively diversified is the sector or industry. With options, you'll mostly be looking at time, price, and volatility. If you're employing the Greeks, you can easily diversify on volatility by seeing what Vega looks like. If you mostly have trades with positive Vega, consider picking up a few that are of negative Vega if you wish to diversify. Vice versa also holds true.

Diversifying by time is easy whether you use the Greeks or not. If you have lots of 30-day trades, consider picking up a few 90-day trades next. Price is another easy one; just choose different strike prices.

How Much Diversification is Too Much?

See the point earlier on getting overly attached to complexity. Keep It Simple, Silly.

Never diversify more than what you can comfortably keep track of. Never get into a trade that you don't know much about (e.g. where it might go, how likely it is to do so), not even to diversify.

Relying Too Much on Buying and Exercising Out-of-the-Money Call Options

Long Calls are a pretty staple move to make as an options trader, but sometimes new traders only think to hang onto them so they can exercise near the expiration date. While this is an option (heh) you can choose with your option, in many cases it can help to buy calls based not on whether or not you think they'll actually be in-the-money before expiration, but based on whether or not you think their premiums will go up in the short-term, whereupon you can immediately sell them all to someone else.

This does of course require taking this move into account with your backtesting, as well as understanding short-term trends, but the point is that you shouldn't overly fixate on only one way of making money with options, when as discussed earlier there are several avenues through which to profit off of them.

Q&A and Summary

Can I ever know too much about options trading?

No. It always helps to gain more knowledge or a broader perspective. This becomes especially true the more you lean on options trading for income.

Is understanding the psychology of my mind important?

Yes. Your mind is what makes all your trading decisions. It's important to be able to step back and see what's prompting you to behave a certain way; facts vs speculation. Careful analysis vs fear. Remember the advice from Chapter 4 on how to help your mind, as this will also help you become more disciplined.

Is complexity always better?

No. Never aim for complexity in or of itself. Keep things simple, and never make something more intricate than it needs to be, or with more moving parts than it needs to have. Generally a highly complex strategy is harder to exit, which means more stress.

What does it mean to stick to my strategy?

It means following the steps of whatever you back tested and analyzed without deviation once you've seen it has a good success rate. What it doesn't mean is refusing to expand into or consider other strategies.

How reliable is the market?

It works how you expect... until it doesn't. You can get a really good idea of what the market will do through analysis, but you can never behave like you can unerringly predict the future. No one is that good.

How important are trade records?

Very. It helps you keep track of what you're doing, and helps you internalize and learn from what you've already done.

How necessary is a trading plan?

It's what allows you to maintain control and composure, as a good plan helps you account for problems you might run into. It prevents you from going into panic mode, and for this reason they're invaluable. They also help you keep your strategies simple but effective by forcing you to describe how you're going to enact them.

What makes up a trading plan?

Know how much you're willing to put into any one trade.

Know where your opportunities are (or research and analyze if you don't yet know).

Know how you're going to get into a trade you want.

Know how you're going to get out of a trade that has succeeded.

Know how you're going to cut your losses and escape from a trade that is going poorly.

Always remember:

- You're not invincible.
- You're not a robot. From time to time you'll make an execution error, especially if you're tired or dehydrated.
- You need to take care of yourself and be patient.
- Never put more money into a trade than what you're comfortable with.

- Volatility is a thing. Options markets can be volatile places. Use your backtests, plans, and analyses to help you respond correctly during a time of volatility.

Chapter 6: Advanced Strategies

Brokers

If you're here, you've processed a heck of a lot of information. Either that, or you're coming from Chapter 3 looking for extra advice on brokers.

This segment is mostly for those who are wondering whether or not to switch brokers, but it also contains advice for those who are on the fence between choosing one broker or another, and don't know which one to go with.

Step 1: Carefully Examine Your Needs

A person's financial needs can change over time, so it doesn't hurt to check in every once in a while. For example, if your trading style involves a high frequency of entering and exiting trades, you likely don't want to remain with a broker who charges you a fee for every trade you make. Rather, you'd want to switch to one that offers a more flat rate.

Likewise, when first starting out you almost certainly would want to prioritize a broker who has a great many educational resources for you to access, along with their own glossaries, and helpful customer support. Brokers that allow you to practice trading in a virtual, no-risk environment would likely also be great for you in these early stages. These so-called "early stages" can last for up to two years, but some traders learn what they need to learn faster, and after a while you might find that the value of easily accessible education and support just isn't worth as much to you anymore, the education you're given not that different from everything you already know.

In that case, as you grow more advanced, you'll want to keep an eye out for brokers who offer more advanced tools for testing, simulation, and probability. You'll want brokers with more in-depth data as well as perhaps the ability to trade in fields other than options.

Be honest with yourself regarding where you are in your trading journey, and what kind of help you need in order to perform better. Generally getting a hold of lots of advanced tools isn't a great idea if you don't have any way to learn how to use them properly.

Even if you believe in being self-taught, you still need to know enough basics before you can know whether you're teaching yourself the correct way or not. In these cases, there is no shame in sticking with a broker who offers professionals to teach or support you.

Step 2: Check Broker Affiliations

Check what regulatory or official bodies this broker has been certified by, or is partnered with. Examples include the Financial Industry Regulatory Authority and the Securities Investor Protection Corporation. These authorities can determine the degree of insurance you get from your broker. Are your trades covered/ insured, for instance, for if the broker company fails? Protection against fraud is another big one to look out for, especially as your trading account becomes more valuable.

Step 3: Check Security

You'll want your broker to have two-factor authentication, like most banks do, especially as your account grows in size. Built-in encryption to protect your earnings also becomes something that you cannot afford to overlook.

Step 4: Check Competition

Some brokers allow you to open free accounts with them. Take advantage of this to get a feel for how other brokers compare to the one you're using now. If you don't have a broker yet, alternatively use this to test-drive a few platforms. Whether you're trading professionally or as a profitable hobby, you want to ensure your platform will support you. If you came here from Chapter 3, I hope you now feel more sure about which broker to go with, as from this point on we're focusing on how to switch.

Step 5: Decide Whether It's Worth Switching Brokers

Generally speaking, if you're reasonably happy with your current broker, you don't need to switch, and in fact having to familiarize yourself with a new platform can be more trouble than it's worth. But if you have gone through the previous four steps and, with research, believe you have found an alternative that'll suit your current (and projected future) needs much better, then you're ready for the next step. Otherwise, just keep carrying on with your current broker. A good guideline for options trading is, "If it ain't broke, don't fix it."

Just like how you don't want to deviate from your strategies willy-nilly, you don't want to change brokers unless you have several strong logical reasons to do so.

Step 6: Make the Switch

To switch brokers, you'll want to be aware of the following:

- If your new broker's customer service isn't willing to help you make the switch, you should reconsider if switching into such apathy is wise
- On the flip side, a competitive broker will offer generous rewards in exchange for you switching to them... while they're nice, don't let them sway you; your new broker still needs to match your present and future needs better than your current broker
- You'll likely be charged a fee by the broker you're leaving

- You can normally move your options contracts over, but it never hurts to ask your new broker-to-be if there are any exceptional circumstances that'd prevent this
- However, transferring these contracts can take a while, potentially causing you to take a hiatus from trading for several days, or even over a week
- You cannot buy or sell during a transfer, so don't do so if there are active trades you need to be able to trade or exercise soon
- You'll almost certainly be asked to provide proof of identity, especially if you're moving from a single account into a joint account (and vice versa)

You'll also likely need to do the following:

1. Any active orders you have running at your current broker (e.g. trade orders or stop-loss orders) need to be canceled. This will save headaches during transference.
2. Request a statement from your current broker, showing your account type and number. It should also show an up-to-date list of your currently held options as well as any other investments you may have.
3. Open your account at your new broker. At some point, you should be asked to fill out a Transfer Initiation Form. If not, ask your new broker if such a form needs to be filled, and how you can do so. Normally these forms are required for your old and new broker to

ensure your account (and all the options it may contain) transfers safely and successfully.

4. After about a week, the transfer should be done. Request a statement from your new broker and carefully compare it to the statement you got from your old broker earlier. This is to help you double-check that your transfer happened correctly, and that you haven't been charged anything you weren't expecting. Unexpected fees or incomplete transfers should be queried as soon as possible.

And it's as simple as that!

You hopefully won't need to switch brokers that often, but when you do this advice will help keep it a worthwhile and relatively hassle-free process.

Swing Trading, Day Trading, and More

First, a quick recap.

Once you're set up with a broker, the basics of swing trading with options are pretty simple:

1. Pick an asset
2. Through research, estimate whether it'll go up or down in value
3. Decide by how much (e.g. roughly what should the strike price be?)
4. Decide how soon (e.g. duration)

5. Enter your trade
6. Decide when to exit, whether with profit or whether to cut a loss

Pretty simple stuff that you already know.

Day trading is much the same process, and both ultimately rely on profiting overall rather than achieving a 100% win rate. However, while swing trades can last for days or months, day trades only last a few hours each if not minutes, and certainly they never last overnight.

From here, the two trading types diverge more and more.

Day Trading vs Swing Trading
Day traders...

- will trade at least 4 times within the course of 5 days
- almost all their trades will be exited before the end of their market's trading day
- though they do use both fundamental and technical analysis, they rely a lot on fundamental analysis in the form of news articles, using the short-term volatility generated in order to trade at a profit
- need a very fast and stable internet connection, as every second can make a huge difference for them
- requires you to be ready to trade in your market the first hour or two when it opens, as that's typically where the best trades happen (check your time zones)

- requires more research and work to be done on a daily basis
- prefers brokers who have a flat rate over those who have commission fees

Swing traders...

- aside from the timeframes mentioned earlier, don't have a set minimum frequency with which they trade
- rely on both fundamental and technical analysis, but with a huge emphasis on technical analysis to follow overall market trends
- it's even possible to remain profitable as a swing trader on technical analysis alone, which can be one way to keep things simple (still I recommend you simplify in other areas first where possible)
- ideally, you'll want to have your research/ analysis done before the market opens on the days you wish to trade; some days you research/ check active trades, some days you actually make new trades
- due to holding fewer trades at once, combined with the reduced reliance on fundamental analysis, do not need to research as much every day, or alternatively have more time and energy to put into researching the few trades they do make
- depending on trading frequency, might prefer commission fees over a flat rate

It's important to note that *neither* is limited just to trading options. Both can be used to trade stocks and other assets directly.

Great Tools and Indicators to Use For Technical Analysis

Here are a few extra things to bear in mind when looking at technical analysis charts:

Candlestick Charts (Tool)

This is an advanced charting technique that allows you to capture an entire day's worth of data in a single bar, known as the 'candlestick.' Coming out of the top and bottom of each bar is a thin line known as the 'wick.' The top of the *wick* tells you the highest price for a stock or asset sold on the market that day, while the bottom end of the *wick* is the lowest.

For a white or green candlestick, the bottom of the *bar* is also the opening price for that trading day, while the top is its closing price. With a black or red candlestick, it's the reverse. In trading, black/ red sticks are used to denote days where the trend was downward, while white/ green sticks denote days when the trend was upward.

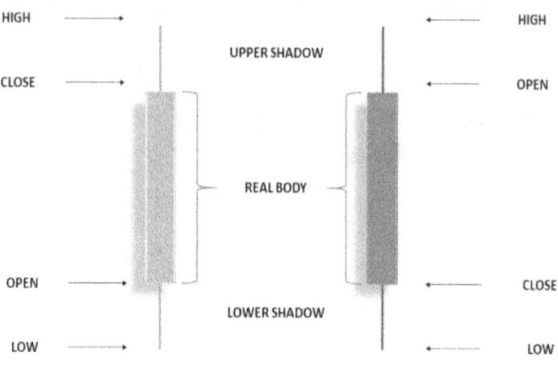

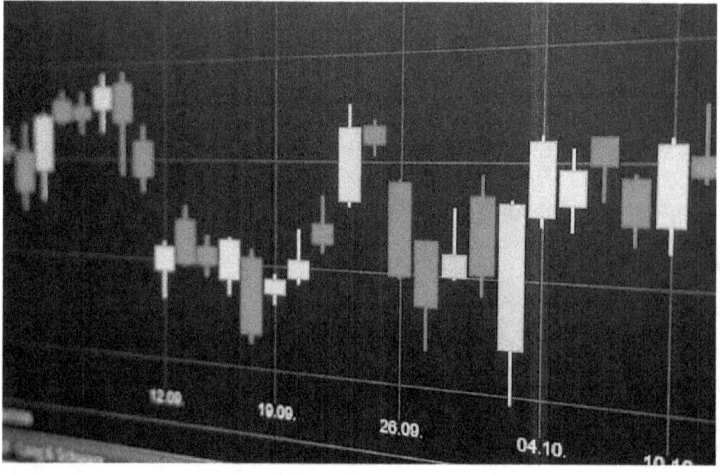

Candlestick charts are the best way to read the indicators below.

The Head and Shoulders Pattern (Indicator)

This is historically one of the most reliable patterns you'll see on your chart. It is a series of trend reversals over time that consist of three crests or high points, with the second crest being the biggest. This big middle crest is the 'head' while the smaller ones before and after it are the 'shoulders.' Between the head and each shoulder is a period where value dips. After the second shoulder, the value just keeps dipping, way down to an extreme low, before the pattern ends and the market cycle begins anew.

What does this pattern tell us?

While you shouldn't assume a chart is going to make the pattern you expect, seeing a crest followed by a dip is a good indicator that you'll see a much bigger crest later on. Likewise, if you see a big crest, followed by a dip, followed by a smaller crest that has already begun dipping down, you know that the trend is just going to continue downwards for a long time before it eventually climbs back up.

Plan your trades accordingly.

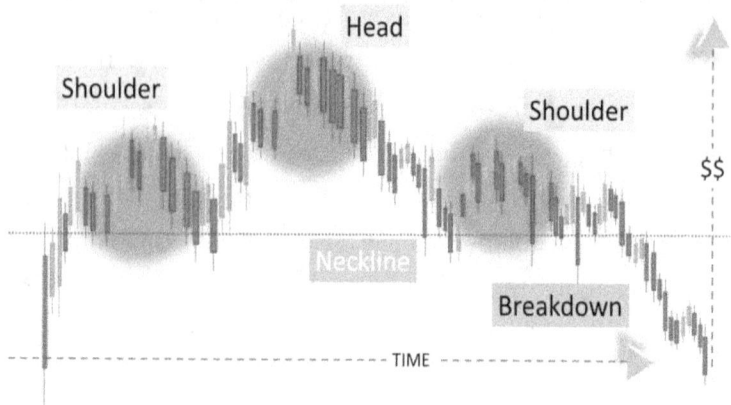

The Cup and Handle (Indicator)

This pattern begins with an upwards trend, peaks, then experiences a very smooth downwards trend; value drops sharply at first, but the rate at which it drops begins to slow. Eventually, this turns into a slow upwards trend, and then a sharp upwards trend, until value returns to roughly what it was when it peaked (before the smooth downward trend). This movement is what we call the 'cup.' If you then see a sharp downward trend, don't be afraid. This is the 'handle.' For a cup that took five months to form, this handle might only last one month, and it indicates a likelihood of a sharp rise in value thereafter. If you spot a potential cup-and-handle, factor it into the rest of your analysis and plan your trades accordingly.

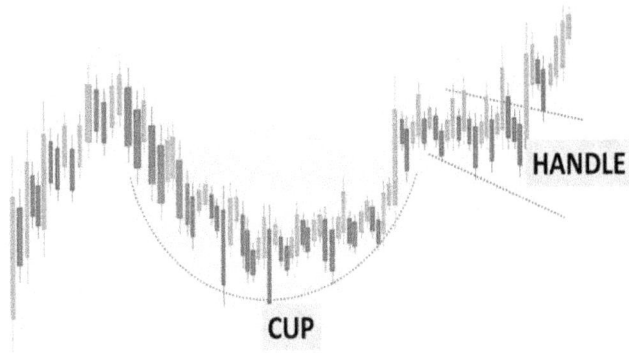

HANDLE

CUP

Three Line Strike (Indicator)

Three black candlesticks followed by a white one. The white bar *usually* opens its trading day lower than the lows of the last three bars, but ends on a high comparable to the high of the first black bar. When this happens, there's an 83% chance that the market will continue on an upward trend. Remember, no one indicator can give an absolute picture.

Three line strike

Three Black Crows (Indicator)

Three black candlesticks, with the opening trade value of each one being lower than the opening value of the previous day. If followed by a white bar (it doesn't have to be), it still closes on a value below that of the opening of the first black bar. This pattern indicates a 78% chance for a downward trend to continue.

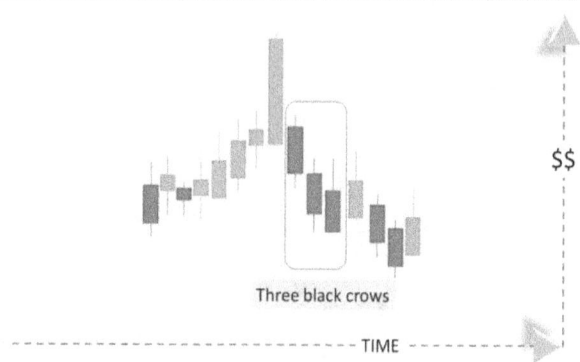

Three black crows

Advanced Tips for Fundamental Analysis

Remember KISS

Quality of data is much more important than quantity. Data is limitless, but you can only use so much. To aid in this, there are two main approaches for Fundamental Analysis.

Top-Down

Here, you're examining things on a country, sector, and industry level. This is where you focus on inflation, commodity prices (whether current or projected), projected GDPs, employment rates, and similar data. This approach is best done to determine whether or not a particular market is even worth trading in.

To do this, pick a type of data (e.g. interest rates), then a type of market that'd be strongly affected by it (e.g. bank stocks, as banks earn a lot through interests). Then, see how they're correlated; see how closely the rise and fall of one matches the rise and fall of another. Often, interest rates and bank stock/ options values are very close, but this cannot be taken for granted. Sometimes bank options values are low even when interest is high, at which point you can then pick one of your other types of sector/ state-level data and compare that to the same market (e.g. employment rates or GDP to the bank market data).

Overall, this helps you build a picture as to what news is relevant, and to what degree it is relevant, when using it to help you make decisions (e.g. during day trading) since you'll have a more solid idea of how different far-reaching factors will affect your market.

Bottom-Up

Best used if you think the economy of a market or country overall might not affect a particular company the way you'd expect. This method doesn't tell you much about the country's economy overall, but does help you get a more intimate picture of a specific company.

This is where you'll focus on the more company-specific information types mentioned under fundamental analysis earlier, such as financial statements and balance sheets.

To do this, first ask yourself how compelling the company's management structure, business model, and brand power is. These are subjective qualities, but if you see that huge quantities of people believe in these qualities, it's a good indicator that it'll prosper and grow even if the economy on a state level isn't doing so well.

More measurable forms of data to include are how much of its profits go into each share it sells (the Earnings-Per-Share). The higher it is, the more profitable it is and the more likely it is to grow.

Another indicator is price-to-earnings, which tells you how much a share pays out compared to what it costs; a low value here is usually a strong indicator of future growth. Extremely high or low values tend to be 'corrected' or moderated faster from being over/ underrated than values that are only moderately higher or lower than normal.

Next is Return-on-Equity, which measures the overall efficiency of a business (a good way to confirm if a business model or management team deserves the faith it has).

Finally, a great bottom-up indicator is the Price-to-Earnings ratio. This is how much a share is worth, divided by how much net worth the business has per share. A value greater than 1 indicates growth, while lower than 1 indicates decline.

If You're a Day Trader...

It's important to note that while you should cover this fundamental research, your "research on a daily basis" will mostly be news and reports once you're satisfied with the top-down/ bottom-up analyses you've done. These analyses, for a day trader, are only there to help you interpret articles or reports, and which ones to watch out for consistently.

Option Tactics for Seasoned Traders

This is a final list of strategies that you can start introducing after a prolonged period of experiencing success, enduring failure, and turning a profit.

The Credit Spread

Also known as a vertical spread. This is the inverse of a debit spread. What you'll do is you'll buy an option with a lower premium and sell one with a higher premium. This starts you out with a profit from the get-go, but will never earn you more than the net premium you get at the start of the trade. It has two main variants, which can be counted as separate strategies:

Short Put Spread

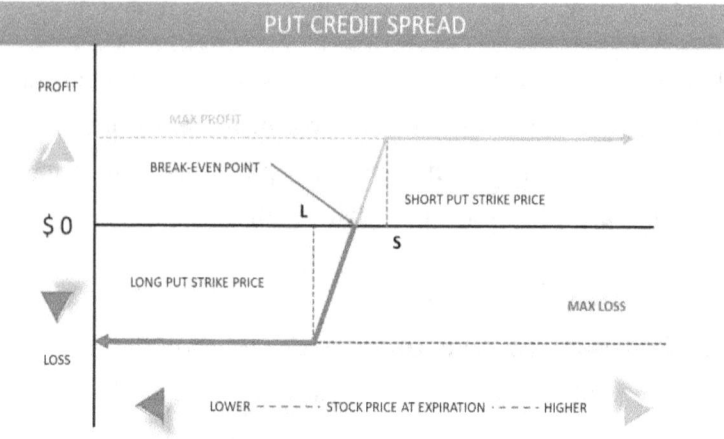

This involves buying a put at a lower strike price (X), and selling another put on the same stock at a higher strike price (Y), both of which should expire in the same month.

At the time you enter with this strategy, you'll usually want the value of your option's stocks to be above strike price Y. You'll typically only enter this strategy when you expect stock values to keep climbing.

This strategy can be an advanced way to safeguard the puts you write. If you don't think you'll be able to buy back the puts you want to sell, entering with this strategy instead means you have also bought puts that at least let you sell the stocks you're obligated to buy for a decent-ish value, cutting costs if the put you sold gets exercised.

Short Call Spread

The second credit spread variant. This involves selling a call at a lower strike price (again, we'll call this X) while selling another call on the same stock at the higher strike price of Y. Again, both should expire within the same month.

Typically, you'll want the value of the attached stocks to be below the value of X, and you'll enter this strategy when you expect market values to decline.

This is similar to making a naked call, which as you'll remember I don't generally recommend.

However, because you also bought Call Y with the caveats mentioned above, it means that there's now a defined upper limit for how much money you'll lose in total if things go wrong. This is because you can use Call Y to ameliorate the losses of an exercised Call X should the stock get much more expensive than you were expecting.

In other words, your maximum loss is only the difference between X and Y (minus your premium of course), as opposed to being theoretically limitless.

This makes going 'naked' more predictable and easier to manage if things go wrong, but the nature of naked calls means I still count this as an advanced strategy even with the safeguard of Call Y in place.

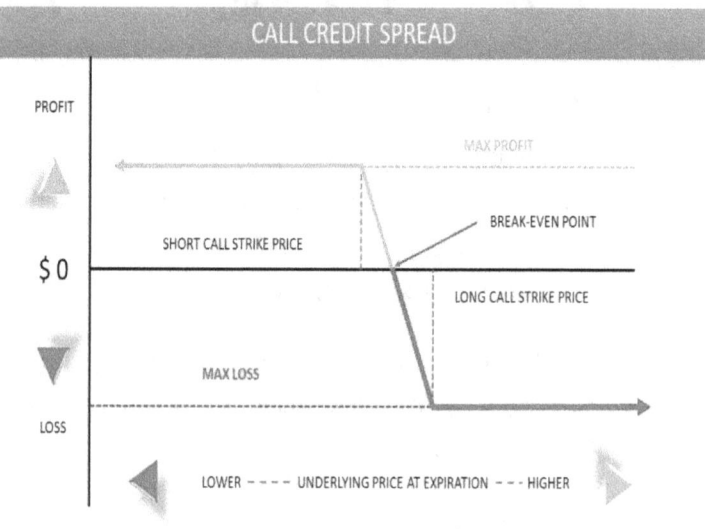

The Iron Condor

Here, you're running a short call spread and a short put spread simultaneously, all as part of one trade.

This is best used if you don't expect the market to move very much at all during the time period set. Now, how do we open this? Let's say for the call spread we have Call X and Call Y, with Y having the higher strike price of the two.

Now, for the put spread we'll have Put A and Put B, with B having the higher strike price of the two. Finally, both your calls should have higher strike prices than the puts.

This is your typical iron condor, and you'll want the value of the attached assets to be somewhere between the strike prices of Put B and Call X. Ideally, bang in the middle, but being a little off is fine.

Then, let all the options expire worthless. This is a great way to get semi-passive income via premiums in a slow-moving, stable market. The call and put you buy as part of the spreads are still both forms of security to help keep your losses predictable, rather than limitless.

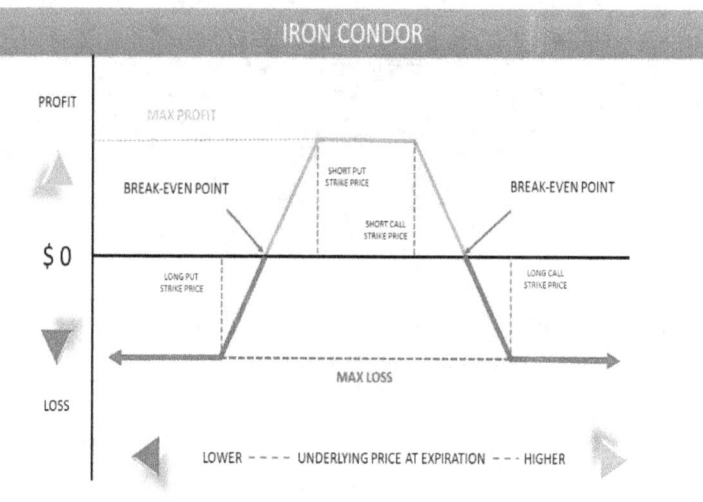

The Iron Butterfly

This is similar to the condor, in that we're taking out two short spreads with the same duration. However, instead of Put A, Put B, Call X, and Call Y, we instead have Put X, Put Y, Call Y, and Call Z.

Yes, this means Put Y and Call Y must have the same strike price, with Call Z's strike being higher, and Put X's being lower. Strike prices must also be the same 'distance' apart from their neighbors. For example, if strike price X = $40 (for example), and strike price Y = $42, then strike price Z must = $44 (X is $2 apart from Y, which is in turn $2 apart from Z).

As another example, if X = $40, but Y = $50, Z would need to be $60 (X is $10 apart from Y, which in turn is $10 apart from Z).

You'll want the asset price to be equal to strike price Y when you enter the trade if you expect little/ no market movement. If you expect the asset price to fall, then make sure it is slightly closer to Z when you start. If you expect it to rise, make sure it is slightly closer to X. You want this trade to expire at Y, as this is what'll earn you the most (your initial premium without any of your sold options being exercised).

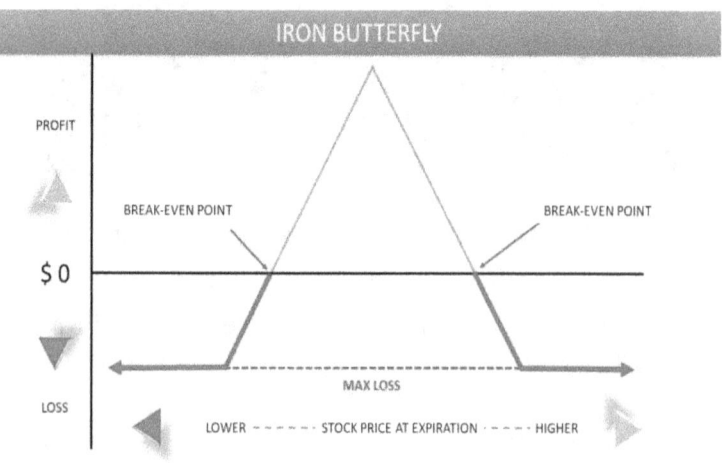

Back Spread Calls

If you have a huge reason to believe that the assets in your market will rise in value, and if the assets themselves are highly volatile, you'll want to run this strategy.

What you want to do is sell a short call spread, then buy an additional call with a strike price of Y. So, you'll have sold one Call X, and have bought two Call Ys.

When you do this, you'll want the value of the asset to be around X when you open the trade. Usually, you'll already have a small profit thanks to the premium from selling Call X, but the longer the duration of your trade, the more likely you are to enter at a debit or initial loss. You also don't want X and Y to be too far apart.

Let's say for example that X here is $40, and Y is $45, and that your underlying asset is about $40 at this time. With this strategy, your maximum loss will occur if your underlying asset moves $5 and now matches strike price Y, as the call you sold will get exercised for the highest it can without you being able to exercise your own (in this case your maximum loss is still only $45 for every share you need to buy in order to fulfill your obligations).

However, if it moves another $5 and becomes $50, then you can exercise your bought calls to break even, and profit becomes theoretically limitless if the prices just keep rising past $50. This is why I say you need to both believe the market will keep rising, as well as believe that the assets are volatile enough to rise a LOT.

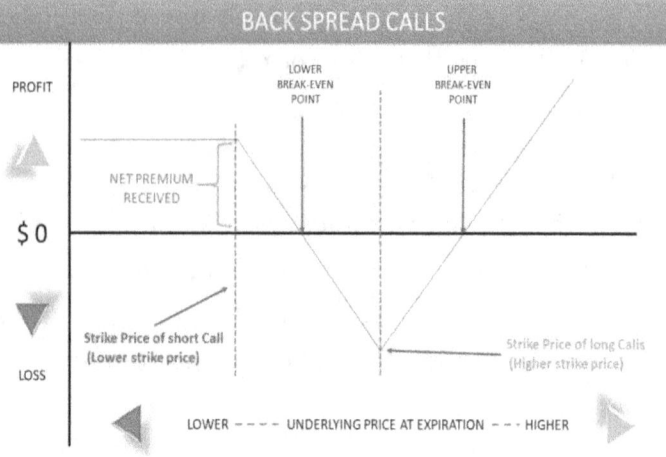

The Long Straddle

Simple to understand, but requires advanced analysis to be done in order to ensure profit.

This strategy requires you to purchase both a call and a put on the exact same assets, with the exact same duration, and the exact same strike prices.

Now, why would we do this? We do this when we believe the price of an asset is going to shift dramatically, but we aren't sure in which direction.

The absolute worst case is if the stock remains exactly the value of the strike price, wherein you still only lose what you paid in premiums.

The best case is to get an extreme change whether in higher value or lower value, wherein you then exercise the options that'll let you earn profit. In theory, there's no limit to how much profit you can earn. It all depends on how big the shift is. Therefore this can be a great choice in volatile markets, or for assets that are about to go from low volatility to high volatility.

To demonstrate how extreme (or not) the change has to be, consider this; a stock from company X is worth $60 per share. A call option exists with a $60 strike price and a premium of $4 per share. A put option with the same duration, and strike price also exists, and to keep things simple we'll say it also has a $4 premium cost per share. To profit, then, share prices would need to change by more than $4+$4=$8 in either direction.

Assuming 100 shares in a single options contract, that's $400 you're paying per contract, for a total of $800. However, if the share price changes from $60 to either $52 or $68, you can break even. If it changes to less than $52 or more than $68, you profit.

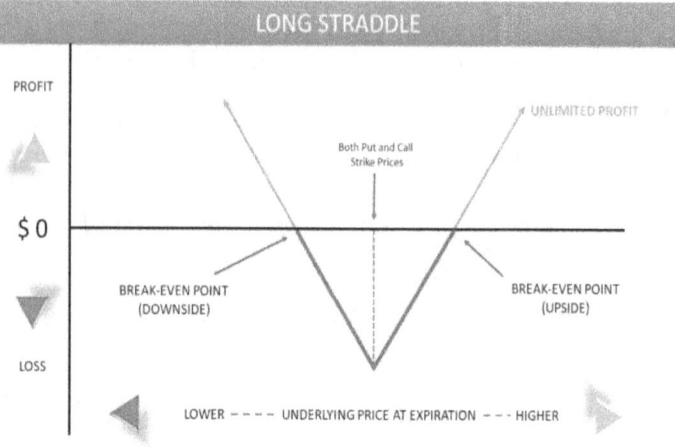

LONG STRADDLE

PROFIT

UNLIMITED PROFIT

Both Put and Call
Strike Prices

$0

BREAK-EVEN POINT
(DOWNSIDE)

BREAK-EVEN POINT
(UPSIDE)

LOSS

LOWER – – – – UNDERLYING PRICE AT EXPIRATION – – – HIGHER

The Long Strangle

A similar name to the Long Straddle, and a similar purpose too. Once again, it's very simple to understand, but demands advanced analysis in order to win out when using it.

The setup is almost exactly like a Straddle, but you're deliberately purchasing options that are well out-of-the-money, and the strike prices don't need to be the same.

The result is a much smaller potential for loss, but also less likelihood of turning a profit unless you're absolutely sure a huge shift is going to happen. An example of this would be an upcoming conference where a minister of health is expected to either endorse or disparage a new food or medicine; a food or medicine that happens to be the underlying asset of your options' stocks.

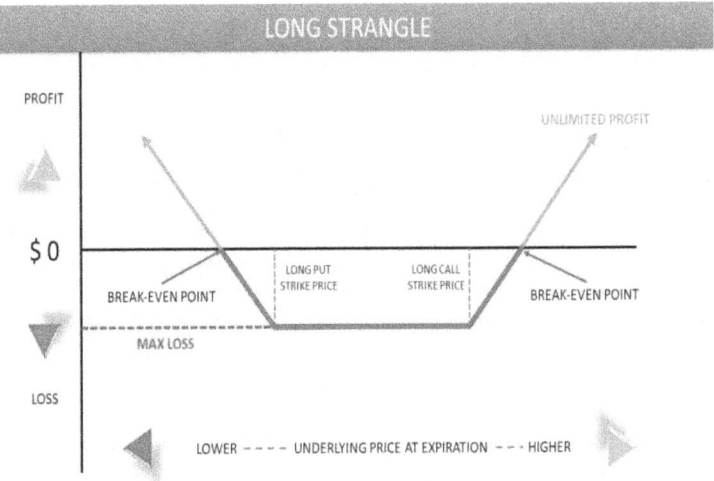

The Short Put

Another deceptively simple strategy, this is where you write a put to someone who owns stocks, giving them the option to sell those stocks to you at the strike price. What makes this an advanced strategy (i.e. not suitable for beginners or even veterans) is that it's purely speculatory; you don't intend to ever actually buy the stock, and you don't have an in-built plan for what to do with that stock.

Maximum loss isn't limitless, but can still be substantial, equaling the total strike price minus the premium you initially got, which is about the same result you'd get from a really bad short call spread.

You'll typically only enter this trade when you know the market hasn't yet reached its distribution cycle. As with all options you write, the most you're getting out of this is the premium you're paid. On the flip side, whoever you wrote the put for usually won't have cause to use it outside of a distribution cycle.

If you're worried they will soon use it, you can offer to buy the puts back to avoid having to buy all their stocks, but expect to pay a higher premium than what you wrote it for in those cases. This is usually because buying it back is a form of cutting your losses.

The one exception is if the assets attached to the put greatly rise in value, reducing the need and premium worth of the put. At that point, remember you can tie up loose ends by offering to buy it back really cheaply, eliminating risk for you while still having earned a net profit.

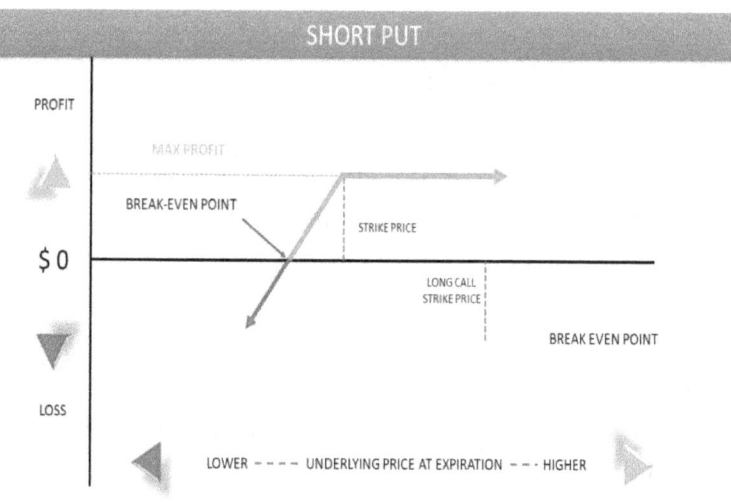

Long Call Butterfly

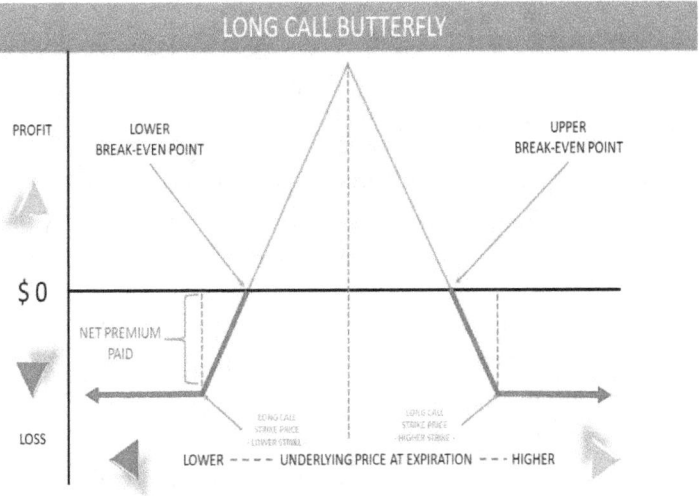

Similar to the Iron Butterfly, but with key differences. You're not taking out two short spreads, but rather you're taking out one short call spread along with a call-based debit spread (see Chapter 3 or overleaf).

This means you'll have bought one Call X (which is in the money already), sold two Calls Y (which are at the money), and bought one Call Z (which is out of the money). Like the Iron Butterfly before, you want the underlying asset of these calls to be at the strike price of Y when you enter, or at least have it be close according to which way you think the market will go. Your maximum profit is achieved if the asset stays equal to strike price Y.

Once again, all these options must have the same expiration date, and be the same distance apart as described in the Iron

Butterfly. This trade is typically a net debit to enter, but makes buying a heavily in-the-money call viable.

While this strategy limits the potential upside of Call X, it makes it profitable to buy in a neutral market, and your potential downsides are limited too. The results from value unexpectedly falling is much better with this strategy than if you just bought X on its own, thanks to the Ys that you sold. Meanwhile, both Z and A helps cover the costs of fulfilling the Ys if they get out of hand.

Naturally, this is best used in a market that won't move much over the duration. Avoid during times of strong growth, decline, or volatility.

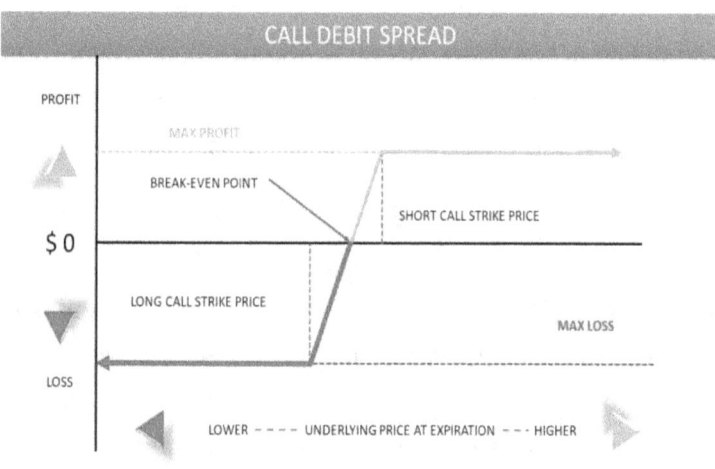

Long Call Condor

Compared to a Long Call Butterfly where all prices and values are equal, the Long Call Condor has a better chance for you to achieve maximum profit... but also has a lower maximum profit ceiling. You trade some potential for a little more consistency.

Here, you are running a short call spread alongside a call-based debit spread, both with the same duration, similar to our previous strategy.

However, instead of three strike prices, we now have four, similar to the Iron Condor, but instead of buying and selling a call, and buying and selling a put, we're just buying two calls and selling two puts.

Your debit spread should involve buying Call A and selling Call B, while your short call spread should involve selling Call X and buying Call Y. Strike Prices should be, in ascending order, A, B, X, Y.

You want your underlying asset to be somewhere between B and X when you open this trade, and once again this trade works best when you predict minimal movement in the market.

Maximum profit is achieved if the asset price stays between B and X, you break even if it falls between either A and B or X and Y, and you lose if it goes past either of those extremes. Due to the way the various options cover one another (e.g. the Y you bought caps the potential losses of the X you sold, and the net value of the A you bought and the B you sold still nets in a profit), your losses are only limited to the initial net premium you paid.

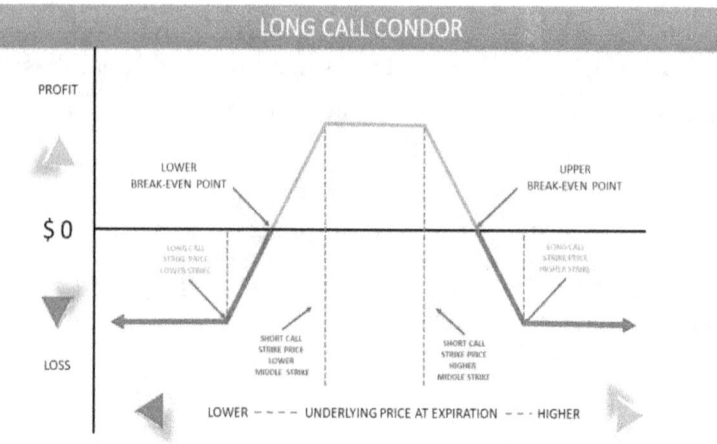

LONG CALL CONDOR

PROFIT

LOWER
BREAK-EVEN POINT

UPPER
BREAK-EVEN POINT

$ 0

LONG CALL
STRIKE PRICE
LOWEST STRIKE

LONG CALL
STRIKE PRICE
HIGHEST STRIKE

SHORT CALL
STRIKE PRICE
LOWER
MIDDLE STRIKE

SHORT CALL
STRIKE PRICE
HIGHER
MIDDLE STRIKE

LOSS

LOWER − − − − UNDERLYING PRICE AT EXPIRATION − − − HIGHER

Conclusion

By now, you have the means to achieve a good understanding of the basic tools and strategies you need to find success in options trading.

You are aware that the biggest mistakes all occur within one's mind, often due to fear or stress, and that while the market dictates what strategies we need to thrive, our composure is ultimately what lets us financially survive no matter what change occurs.

However, as stated all the way back in Chapter 4, you don't know what you don't know. You're now more than ready to start as a rookie, and to keep yourself protected through operating in small, simple trades. You've also been shown advanced strategies with tips on where you'd use them. That said, remember one of the biggest traps of all: the lie of invincibility. Never fall for it. Never let a booming market fool you into neglecting yourself or your financial protection. Never forget to mitigate risks using tools like the 1-5% rule, or even spreads like the debit spread which you could likely use happily now, or the credit spread variants once you're more seasoned and comfortable.

Never neglect all these tools you have, and don't be shy about learning more about how to use them, whether through your broker or through a trusted advisor. There's an old adage among pilots that goes, "90% of a successful landing is in the setup."

Among options traders, that setup is your backtesting. It's your broker's data and educational facilities. It's your fundamental analysis. It's your technical analysis. It's your hydration. It's your sleep schedule. It's everything that lets you be the most knowledgeable and attentive trader you can be.

Without that, you'll never know for sure if your strategies will land. You can only guess. Or gamble.

But trading isn't meant to be treated as a gamble, at least not in the way that most people treat gambling. This isn't a game to be won, so much as a craft to be perfected and enjoyed. Yes, enjoyed, as the extra income makes stepping towards financial freedom that much easier. But also respected, as what you risk to reach that dream is still very real, and the money you choose to put in must be done with the greatest care.

Whether you choose to continue this trade as a vocation or as a side-hustle, you'll notice that it takes a good deal of initial energy to get rolling. But after that, you'll find the overall trend is that it becomes smoother with experience, and the unexpected losses or market changes that used to scare you in your rough beginning months or years will, more and more, only make you glance and think, "Oh, I've seen this before, and after perhaps falling over a few times I now know just what to do."

If you enjoyed this book, please let me know what you made of it with an honest review. Walking through the world of options trading is a weird and wonderful experience, and I thank you for sharing it with me.

References

Ally. (2020, September 16). *Trading vs. investing: What's the difference?* Ally: A Community for Your Financial Well-Being. https://www.ally.com/do-it-right/investing/trading-vs-investing/#:~:text=While%20the%20terms%20are%20often

Banton, C. (2019a, October 11). *How much money do you need to start trading?* Investopedia. https://www.investopedia.com/ask/answers/08/minimum-amounts-of-money-to-start-trading.asp

Banton, C. (2019b, December 11). *The importance of time value in options trading.* Investopedia. https://www.investopedia.com/articles/optioninvestor/02/021302.asp

Bryant, S. (2019, December 3). *Is it risky to invest in options?* Investopedia. https://www.investopedia.com/articles/investing/122815/it-risky-invest-options.asp

Capre, C. (2018, December 4). *How to trade for a living without much capital.* 2ndSkiesForex. https://2ndskiesforex.com/trading-strategies/forex-strategies/how-to-trade-for-a-living-without-much-capital/

CFI Education. (2021). *Option Greeks - learn how to calculate the key Greeks metrics.* Corporate Finance Institute. https://corporatefinanceinstitute.com/resources/knowledge/trading-investing/option-greeks/

Chen, J. (2021, February 19). Day trader. Investopedia. https://www.investopedia.com/terms/d/daytrader.asp

Davis, C. (2020, November 20). *Options trading for beginners: Strategies for getting started.* NerdWallet. https://www.nerdwallet.com/article/investing/options-trading-101

Downey, L. (2021, February 10). *10 options strategies to know.* Investopedia. https://www.investopedia.com/trading/options-strategies/

Earn2Trade. (2020, May 12). *Fundamental analysis - A complete guide from basic to advanced.* Earn2Trade Blog. https://blog.earn2trade.com/fundamental-analysis/

Evdakov, S. (2019, February 14). *How option traders can diversify & minimize their risk ep 223.* Tradersfly. https://tradersfly.com/blog/option-traders-diversify-ep-223/

Farley, A. (2021, January 7). *The 5 most powerful candlestick patterns*. Investopedia. https://www.investopedia.com/articles/active-trading/092315/5-most-powerful-candlestick-patterns.asp

Fidelity's Trading Strategy Desk. (2021). *7 common options trading mistakes*. Fidelity. https://www.fidelity.com/learning-center/investment-products/options/7-common-options-mistakes

Folger, J. (2020, January 16). *Investing vs. trading: What's the difference?* Investopedia. https://www.investopedia.com/ask/answers/12/difference-investing-trading.asp

Forex Alchemy Administration. (2014, April 24). *10 things you can do right now to build patience while trading. #5 will change your life, as well as your trading*. Forex Alchemy. https://www.forexalchemy.com/10-things-you-can-do-right-now-to-build-patience-while-trading-5-will-change-your-life-as-well-as-your-trading

Frederick, R. (2020, May 19). *How to understand option Greeks*. Schwab Brokerage. https://www.schwab.com/resource-center/insights/content/how-to-understand-options-greeks

George, D. (2020, February 24). *When and how to switch online brokerages*. The Motley Fool. https://www.fool.com/the-ascent/buying-stocks/articles/when-how-switch-online-brokerages/

Hall, M. (2019, November 13). *Market cycles: The key to maximum returns*. Investopedia. https://www.investopedia.com/trading/market-cycles-key-maximum-returns/

Investopedia Staff. (2021, January 28). *The ins and outs of selling options*. Investopedia. https://www.investopedia.com/articles/optioninvestor/09/selling-options.asp

Jackson, A.-L. (2021, February 1). *Options vs. stocks: Which is right for you?* NerdWallet. https://www.nerdwallet.com/article/investing/options-vs-stocks

Kowalski, C. (2020, March 12). *What's the right time to buy a call option?* The Balance. https://www.thebalance.com/buying-a-call-option-809142

Kuepper, J. (2019, June 25). *The importance of backtesting trading strategies*. Investopedia.

https://www.investopedia.com/articles/trading/05/030205.asp

Kuepper, J. (2020, June 10). *The daily routine of a swing trader*. Investopedia. https://www.investopedia.com/articles/trading/06/dayofswingtrader.asp

LAT Staff. (2020, March 5). *The four pillars of trading*. London Academy of Trading. https://www.lat.london/news-resources/news-blog/the-four-pillars-of-successful-trading/

Milton, A. (2020, October 29). *How and why to use a covered call option strategy*. The Balance. https://www.thebalance.com/short-covered-call-1031344

Mitchell, C. (2020a, April 22). *Writer*. Investopedia. https://www.investopedia.com/terms/w/writer.asp#:~:text=What%20Is%20an%20Option%20Writer

Mitchell, C. (2020b, June 29). *Definitions of long, short, bullish, and bearish*. The Balance. https://www.thebalance.com/what-do-long-short-bullish-and-bearish-mean-1030894

Nickolas, S. (2020, September 28). W*hat's the difference between a credit spread and a debit spread?* Investopedia. https://www.investopedia.com/ask/answers/042215

/whats-difference-between-credit-spread-and-debt-spread.asp

Picardo, E. (2021, January 28). *The basics of options profitability.* Investopedia. https://www.investopedia.com/articles/active-trading/091714/basics-options-profitability.asp#:~:text=Basics%20of%20Option%20Profitability

Sanlam Reality. (2016). *How to attain financial freedom in our modern world.* Sanlam Reality. https://www.sanlamreality.co.za/wealth-sense/what-does-financial-freedom-mean-in-todays-world/

Schmidt, D. (2019, June 12). *How to start swing trading options.* Benzinga. https://www.benzinga.com/money/swing-trading-options/

Summa, J. (2021, February 23). *Option greeks: The 4 factors to measure risk.* Investopedia. https://www.investopedia.com/trading/getting-to-know-the-greeks/#the-greeks

Teo, R. (2020, October 28). *How to backtest a trading strategy even if you don't know coding.* TradingwithRayner. https://www.tradingwithrayner.com/how-to-backtest-a-trading-strategy/

The Options Guide. (2017). *Debit spreads*. The Options
    Guide.
    https://www.theoptionsguide.com/debit-spread.aspx

Thinktrade. (2006). *Advantages and disadvantages of
    options*. Thinktrade.
    https://www.thinktrade.net/options-advantages-
    and-disadvantages.php

Trading Strategy Guides. (2021, February 10). *Swing trading
    strategies that work*. Trading Strategy Guides.
    https://tradingstrategyguides.com/swing-trading-
    strategies-that-work/

Vermeulen, C. (2021, February 13). *5 reasons why people
    prefer to trade options over stocks*. FX Empire.
    https://www.fxempire.com/forecasts/article/5-
    reasons-why-people-prefer-to-trade-options-over-
    stocks-700252

Yochim, D. (2017, May 26). *Risks and benefits of trading
    options*. NerdWallet.
    https://www.nerdwallet.com/blog/investing/options
    -trading-risks-benefits/

Images

165106. (2018). Coffee Cappuccino Drink Espresso Caffeine.
    In *Pixabay*.
    https://pixabay.com/photos/coffee-cappuccino-
    drink-espresso-3842200/

Altmann, G. (2015). Stock Exchange Bull Bear Securities
Market Shares. In *Pixabay*.
https://pixabay.com/illustrations/stock-exchange-
bull-bear-securities-642896/

Altmann, G. (2017a). Businessman Businessmen Success
Arrow Profit Boom. In *Pixabay*.
https://pixabay.com/illustrations/businessman-
businessmen-success-2241421/

Altmann, G. (2017b). Recession Economy 3d Man Magnifying
Glass Analysis. In *Pixabay*.
https://pixabay.com/photos/recession-economy-3d-
man-2530816/

Free-Photos. (2016). Reading Bookworm Man Books
Learning Literature. In *Pixabay*.
https://pixabay.com/photos/reading-bookworm-
man-books-1246520/

Hassan, M. (2019). Risk Money Cliff Chasing Run Trying
Catch Hook. In *Pixabay*.
https://pixabay.com/illustrations/risk-money-cliff-
chasing-run-4423433/

Hausmann, K. (2017). Stone Age painting mural Lascaux cave
paintings. In *Pixabay*.
https://pixabay.com/photos/stone-age-painting-
mural-lascaux-2115390/

Lachmann-Anke, P., & Lachmann-Anke, M. (2015). Refugees Economic Migrants Financial Equalization. In *Pixabay*. https://pixabay.com/photos/refugees-economic-migrants-1015305/

Mingkhwun, B. (2019). Marketing Graph Screen Exchange Communication. In *Pixabay*. https://pixabay.com/photos/marketing-graph-screen-exchange-4596064/

Nekrashevich, A. (2021). Pen Business Eyewear Research. In *Pexels*. https://www.pexels.com/photo/pen-business-eyewear-research-6801648/

OpenClipart-Vectors. (2013). Bear Animal Brown Silhouette Brown Animals. In *Pixabay*. https://pixabay.com/vectors/bear-animal-brown-silhouette-160226/

Piacquadio, A. (2020). Woman in Red T-shirt Looking at Her Laptop. In *Pexels*. https://www.pexels.com/photo/woman-in-red-t-shirt-looking-at-her-laptop-3755761/

PIX1861. (2017). Chart Trading Courses Analysis Candlestick. In *Pixabay*. https://pixabay.com/photos/chart-trading-courses-analysis-1942060/

Pixabay. (2016). Chess Piece. In *Pexels*.
https://www.pexels.com/photo/battle-black-blur-board-game-260024/

Pixabay. (2017). Pile of Folders. In *Pexels*.
https://www.pexels.com/photo/batch-books-document-education-357514/

Socha, A. (2017). Question Mark Pile Questions Symbol Ask Help. In *Pixabay*.
https://pixabay.com/illustrations/question-mark-pile-questions-symbol-2492009/

Son, H. (2020). Blue and Black Butterfly on Persons Hand. In *Pexels*.
https://www.pexels.com/photo/blue-and-black-butterfly-on-persons-hand-5293162/

Teoh, J. (2018). Ancient Greek Temple. In *Pexels*.
https://www.pexels.com/photo/ancient-greek-temple-951531/

Vlasceanu, M. (2018). High-rise Building. In *Pexels*.
https://www.pexels.com/photo/high-rise-building-1400249/

wrupcich. (2015). Condor Flight Sky Peru Flying. In *Pixabay*.
https://pixabay.com/photos/condor-flight-sky-peru-flying-943300/